BEYOND THE MAKEUP

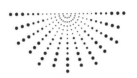

BEYOND THE MAKEUP

MY GUIDE FOR BALANCING SELF, FAITH, FAMILY, AND LOVE

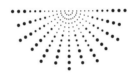

LAKERTISHA SLADE MCIVER

To my beautiful family; I am nothing without you. It's your love and support that keeps me on the comeback!

This book is for you.

To Jevon, my Loving Husband, and our children, Brianna, Kalie, Nick, Jasmine, Jaylen, Jevon Jr., and Jade, I love you immensely. I'm thankful that you've challenged me to become better. To my dad Herman "NIP" Slade, there isn't a day that goes by that I don't miss you. To my mom, Mary, you are the best mom in the world. You taught me how to love with compassion and how to always overcome obstacles. To my siblings—Shavelle, Randolph, Donavus, Chantea, and Hysha (my sister–cousin), thank you and I love you dearly and will always cherish our fond memories. My nephew and niece, Marcus and NaPorsha, both of you give me life and I am grateful for your unselfish love. To my youngest nephew and niece, Dillon and Aniya, keep setting goals and following your dreams. To my godmother, Audrey and my godfather, Richard - I love you for loving me unconditionally. To the rest of my family, you are all my favorites, and have given me reason to grow.

To my many friends – you've inspired me, prayed for me, challenged me, and encouraged me along the way on this awesome journey. You all are very valuable to me and add value to my life. Just let me say that your hunger for the truth is what keeps me authentic and transparent. I will always live in my own truth because without the truth, I would not be the woman I am today.

CONTENTS

Foreword by Dr. Gloria Mayfield Banks

Lakertisha Slade Mciver fully inhabits every space of herself with no pretense and no apologies. She is confidence personified. When you walk into a room and she's there, you know it. She doesn't blend into the background, and she doesn't overshadow those around her. She is the perfect balance of grace, style, and class.

As her Elite Executive National Sales Director and mentor, I've had the privilege to watch her grow and triumph in many areas. Lakertisha is undeniably authentic and determined. She is relentless in her pursuit of reaching her goals and leaving a legacy for her family. My team knows that I want them to use their gifts, Live Out LOUD and not hide in the shadows. I teach them that their skill set will come from preparation and practice. In order to go up, you have to show up.

In the title of this book and throughout its pages, Lakertisha challenges you to live a full and impactful life while rising above challenges, learning from mistakes, and nurturing positive relationships. The lesson is to push through. Push when things are difficult. Push when you are not comfortable. Push when you want to grow. You will get better. You will grow. You will find your path. You will become the queen you are meant to be.

Foreword by Bishop Walter Gwin

Life is to be lived not feared. No matter what station you hold on this planet, life is to be lived, and lived big. The advice columnist Ann Landers stated, "Nobody gets to live life backward. Look ahead ... that is where your future lies." Sure, there will be struggles, yes you will fall from time to time, people will not always accept your method of transport, nor will they all agree with your views. But one thing you can never do is give up in your quest for living life big and finishing strong.

After observing Lakertisha over her years of service in our church, how she loves God, interacts with people as equals, patiently and lovingly serves her husband and children, I can tell you that the authenticity that she brings to the conversation is impeccable. She reveals practice over theory using her uncanny methodology. She allows her readers to take a look behind the curtains of her life, exposing her vulnerabilities, her failures--as well as her victories--while beckoning them to somehow draw the strength and vision necessary to win at all cost.

This presentation of her storied life allows others to believe that they too can experience a more full, impactful, productive existence as they feel the fear of living. This book is unique because it highlights the enormous role played by persistence, patience, and love on both the home front and in the business world. It shows how—by developing a winning attitude—it is possible to manage the pressures of both worlds to such a degree that you are able to perform on extraordinary levels.

Who would have thought Lakertisha would be able to survive all of the obstacles she endured, and produce such an artistic masterpiece you are holding in your hand? And the greater question is: why would she take the time to share so much of her life the way she does in such an overly judgmental society? Well the answer is simple. First and foremost, Lakertisha stands on one of her favorite verses in the Bible, Jeremiah 29:11: "For I know the plans I have for you, declares the LORD, plans to prosper you and not to harm you, plans to give you hope and a future."

Finally, she wrote this book because Lakertisha believes she was placed on this planet to make a difference in the lives of others and to leave the world better than she found it. High achievers do more than merely cope with pressure, they live for it, in fact, they thrive on it. In my opinion, this author is one-in-a-million and there is no more of an impressive work than that in which you are holding. Great work, Lakertisha Mciver, and thank you being "The Comeback Queen" and giving the world, *Beyond The Makeup.*

#Tishtalk

At varied points in this book, you will find pages marked with #TISHTALK. These are your exercises and homework to help you on your journey to becoming your best self. So do the work, the book is set up for you to keep a record of it all and see where you go in this journey.

BEYOND THE MAKEUP

It happened so fast. He told me not to scream. He had a knife to my back, and told me to walk. My friends were at the bar having drinks. Being a non-drinker, I had decided to wait for them at the pool. Just a few feet away, my friends were having the time of their life, and I was about to fight for mine.

My senior year in college and it was spring break. My friends and I (we called ourselves the 5 Pack) were excited about getting ready to graduate from the *illustrious,* North Carolina A&T State University. It was an all-girls trip, and we were vacationing in Jamaica; enjoying the white sandy beaches, perfect weather, and the clear blue water. We were young, single, and carefree. It was our last night on the island, and we stepped out looking good, smelling good, and feeling good. I just knew it was going to be a night to remember. It was.

I woke up in a small room, beaten and bloody. I had been kidnapped by a demented, deranged, man. He had singled me out from my friends; told me that I was his supermodel girlfriend. He picked me for my looks but admitted that he was surprised by my strength. "Damn, I picked the wrong one. You're much stronger than I thought." I was fighting for my life, but the more I fought, the more it infuriated him.

He vowed to cut me up into little pieces and sprinkle my body parts all over the island. I knew I had to think quickly. I had to find a way out. I refused to become a statistic. The only thing I kept thinking of is my family would never be able to find me if I don't get away because he was very crazy and deranged. I knew I had to come up with a plan; the things he kept saying clued me in that he was evil and possessed by a demon. I begged him to let me go to the bathroom to make my face pretty again. After all, supermodels don't have bloody faces. He finally agreed, and I discovered a tiny window in the bathroom. It was just big enough for me to shimmy through. I never ran so fast in my life.

Since I escaped and broke free, I knew what I was going to do. I would spend the rest of my life being as bold and fabulous as I could. I would spend the rest of my life shining a light so bright, even that girl locked in that tiny room would feel it. And I would make sure everyone else could as well. That moment, of being held by a mad man would be the smallest part of my life, for from the depths of hell truly beautiful things can rise.

And I would definitely be the most beautiful thing of all.

I've had several instances in my life where I was forced to face something head-on. Life is for the living and as the saying goes, life happens. As a former athlete, I know either you control the ball, or the ball controls you. To win the game or in life, you need to maintain some level of control.

When I speak to audiences, I share my remarkable journey of a kidnapped college student to business prominence, with stops along the way as a college basketball athlete, educator, mentor, and entrepreneur. I share my ability to bounce back in any situation. Of course, I'm privileged and proud to claim my most important titles and roles of mother, wife, daughter, sister, and friend.

Growing up, I was always *that kid* who gave advice, who was the voice of reason. My mom can attest to the fact that I seemed like a little adult trapped in a child's body—and might I add, wearing the latest fashion. I was the "different" child. I loved doing hair, playing in makeup, painting my nails and I loved jewelry. I always wanted to be "dressed up."

While growing up, I saw my mother work two jobs for twenty-five years, making sacrifices for me and my siblings, and I knew in my heart that I would be successful because of her strength. My mother is one of those "give it to you straight" types of moms. If you don't want to know the truth, don't ask Mary Slade.

I'm sure my mom's straightforward approach rubbed off on me. It's not always easy to face a situation or person head-on, but sometimes, it is necessary to go forward. I've had to deal with numerous uncomfortable situations and people—especially the people, but I learned from Mom that I could only take responsibility for me. She'd say, "You can't control the situation, only how you react to it." She would also say, "People may not like you, and it's okay as long as you like and love yourself."

I want this book to embody my passion for fashion, my faith, my family, my friendships, and my truth which is yes, I am a "Dollar Making Diva" who came up from the North Carolina red clay, because we didn't have grass in my front yard off West Blvd in Charlotte, NC. It was that red dirt that made me who I am today. I made it out of the hood and became successful in my own right from making smart decisions, some the hardest of my life. Most importantly, I kept my faith, believed that I could have it all – the glitter, glitz, glamour, family, while balancing school and a career. It was rough but making goal posters and vision boards helped me see my way through and I want you to learn from me, to operate in your gift and discover your hidden talents.

I'm still here, and these principles are the reasons why:

1. **The F Words.** I can say without a doubt that the woman I am today is because of my faith, family, and friends. To say that my life has been filled with blessings is an understatement – serving a big God who never fails, a strong family bond, and a phenomenal group of friends who support and keep me grounded. Success in life means nothing if you don't have beautiful people to hug, cry or celebrate your victories.

2. **Face the Mirror.** There have been many times in my life when I haven't liked my current situation. What did I do? I changed it. I had to do it for myself. I had to look in the mirror and accept the woman staring back.

3. **Start With the Right Face.** I learned how to face my situation head-on and then make a change. If you don't like where you are, no one else is going to fix it for you. Change starts with you.

4. **Create Good Habits.** People are always commenting and complimenting me on my positivity: I'm smiling, encouraging someone, giving out what I would like to get back. If you make something a habit (a good habit), it becomes a part of you.

5. **Drive Out Drama.** "You are what you attract." I've heard this saying many times, but recently, I had to stop and think about what it really means to me. I know I am blessed with a loving and supportive husband, smart, well-mannered kids, and the most amazing friends a girl could ask for. I don't believe this is an accident or a fluke, or even, dare I say the word … luck. I feel this is truly a result of reaping what I sow and sowing what I reap.

6. **The "Walk-in" Closet.** The "walk-in" closet is not just for clothes. It's a one size fits all kind of closet. It's a meditation and prayer room, an intimate, extra cozy café built for two, and lastly, it's a great snuggle spot. Your closet doesn't do all that? Let me show how to make the conversion.

7. **Be a Businesswoman and Not a Busy Woman.** Growing up, I had many strong role models, both male and female. Of course, I gravitated towards the women in my life who were amazing mothers and showed me how to be loving, kind, and God-fearing soul. It wasn't until I went to college and met the incomparable Ann Shears would I understand how to be a businesswoman. It was under her tutelage that I learned the principles of business.

8. **Start Tripping.** I love to travel. I wrote a good portion of this book while traveling. Every time I got on an airplane, whether first-class or coach, my pen would become a magic wand. Writing is therapeutic for me. Traveling is my classroom. I have

a chance to meet so many interesting people from all over the world. I learn from them and their experiences. This keeps me from being stagnant and to start each day anew. It also helps me to remember how blessed my life is, even when I am fighting through the worst of days.

I deliver motivational speeches, set up workshops, provide glamour consultations, organize and model in fashion shows and provide pampering seminars to make women and men feel and look good. My goal is to share with you why I wholeheartedly believe that you can become your best self.

So, let's get started.

1

THE F WORDS

My life is filled with F words. No, I don't mean the bad F words, the good ones. My first "F word" is faith. Jevon and I have based our marriage on faith. We have been faithful to God's word, and he has blessed our family and our lives with an abundance of love. My second "F word" is family. We have a big, beautiful, and loving family. Our children range from young adults to teenagers. We've weathered many storms and celebrated many triumphs, but most of all, we've done it together. My last "F Word" is friendship. I have an amazing, core group of friends who have known me for twenty plus years. They are from different walks of life and provide different perspectives of life as well. We are each other's sounding boards and counselors. We have an unbreakable bond that has allowed us to be there in the highs and lows in life. Even if we disagree, we are still mature enough to know losing our friendship is non-negotiable.

I will never forget the day I met my husband. In fact, the memory of how it all played out still lives fresh in my mind. I had recently graduated from North Carolina A&T State University with nothing but conquering the world on my mind. I felt as if nothing could hold me back from my dreams. It was a damp and sunny morning in the great city of Charlotte. I had a feeling inside of me that day was going to be different from any other. I remember feeling extremely hungry that morning, but because I had my Mary Kay appointment in the afternoon, I knew that I needed to eat breakfast. I know that you may be thinking, "Well it is morning and you should have felt hungry." However, I am not talking about a regular craving for a meal. I felt as if I had the not eaten in days kind of hungry.

As I drove down a familiar street that I had traveled many times, I remembered there was a restaurant just around the corner. I didn't really want to go there because after being away at school, my taste buds had changed. I guess you could say that I had gotten spoiled going to some four- and five-star restaurants, the white linen tablecloth type of restaurants. However, my stomach was growling louder than my ability to rationalize about the type of food I was about to consume. I thought to myself, *I guess I'll just get something to tide me over until later.* Little did I know the turn I was about to take would change my life forever.

I got out of my car and was immediately weary as I saw the line stretching around the lobby almost to the door. I groaned with anxiety. I caught myself and calmed down. The truth of the matter was I wasn't going anywhere else, as hungry as I felt. I waited and waited as the line grew shorter and shorter. Finally, I made it to the counter to give my order. The restaurant was soul food, cafeteria style. As I looked at all the home-style choices, it was like being in my mother's kitchen, and the smell of the food coming from the steam tables was enticing.

As I made my approach, each server asked me what I'd like, and as I told them, they piled it high on the plate and moved me forward assembly line style with a cadence of "Next, may I help you?" As I was waiting in line to get to the counter to pay, I was tempted to start eating my food in line. Yes, I know, ratchet.

I was unaware I had made it to the cash register, my head buried in my purse searching the different compartments looking for my payment, I heard a voice say, "Good Afternoon, that will be $11.75."

Without looking up at the male voice and frustrated because I had reached the check-out counter so fast, "Give me a minute please."

"Take all the time you need," the voice responded. That voice sent

2

shockwaves through my body. I will never forget it as long as I live. I remember He was so calm, cool and collected. I finally found my money and as I looked up, it was if I was frozen in the moment. I remember that I had to gather myself because it felt like déjà vu. *Had I been here before?* Why did it feel like the man smiling back at me had been in my dreams?

You guessed it ... this man would become my loving husband, Jevon.

I can't remember, but he says I was smiling from ear to ear. His recollection, not mine. I just remember being cocky and saying okay and asking for a lemonade, too. He offered to throw in a dessert since he thought I looked so sweet.

Was this dude flirting with me? Yes! I was giggling on the inside. I kept thinking; I *know he is not flirting with me from behind this counter.*

"What's your name?" His voice was smooth and steady.

"Why?" I replied with a slight 'tude. I didn't want to let him know I was remotely fazed by his flirting. He didn't stop there. He asked me to go out on a date, and to paint the picture, there was a long line of people waiting to pay for their food and this rough around the edges but sweet, spirited gentleman was asking for my name and even walked me out of the restaurant. Walked me to my car and asked for a kiss on the first day he met me, Really he was 'shooting his shot' and I was flattered right away by his boldness I have always liked a man that knows what he likes, or wants and goes after it.

That's right; he left the register with a line of people waiting! Of course, now I know that someone else picked up his slack and took over his duties.

Well, I was just astonished that this man was so intrigued with me, that he would walk me all the way outside to my car and ask for my telephone number and a kiss. Yes, he was so bold he asked me for my name again, my number to contact me to take me out, and a kiss the very first day. He said he knew it was love at first sight. I was thinking this dude is crazy, and to mess with his ego a little bit I told him that I did not date the help. Although, I was very flattered, I had just graduated from college and was only interested in dating career types or college graduates, so I thought. He was a very successful entrepreneur ---a type I hadn't considered.

To my surprise, he was unfazed by my "dating the help" quip and still wanted to know my name. I gave in and told him, "Tisha but my friends call me Tish."

He said, "No. What's your real name?" He went on to explain God had shown him his wife in a vision and said she had a complicated name. I told him my full name was Lakertisha Slade, and he said he knew I was the one God had promised.

"Wow," was all I could say. Then, after I gathered myself, I looked at him like hmmm, this brother is fine and has a nice muscular build. He intrigued me because he was intelligent and seemingly easy going. I had been judging him instead of looking at the man before me. I was acting uppity and my dream man was standing right in front of me asking for a kiss.

I told him if he was serious, he would find me and come to my house with a dozen roses. Guess what? He found me, and 23 years of marriage later, seven children, six grandchildren, and more than 50 vacations, we are still making it do what it do. Baby, I love me some him.

Did the roses get him a kiss? A lady never kisses and tells.

I do believe my favorite trait to love about my husband is how he values family. He is family oriented and always has been. Coming from a family of love and faith, I value family as well. So, when we decided to get married, it was not a big issue to merge our family values together. In fact, I think that's the core that keeps our family going. Although, we are very traditional in some ways, we are very modern in others.

I love the fact that we celebrate birthdays like "National Holidays" in our family. We have always loved celebrating one another and when it's your special day, you get the movie star treatment.

Growing up, I remember that my parents made a big deal out of birthdays and Valentine's Day. No one was left out. My brother always got candy on Valentine's Day, too.

As young children, my siblings and I were heavily involved in sports. My parents never missed a football or basketball game, a track meet or cheerleading event. They made sure they were in the stands or the audience cheering us on and giving us praise. My mom worked a full-time and a part-time job for a while, so she was working, and my dad was the caretaker during those times. They were an amazing team who made sure we didn't lack for anything. As a family, we would go to my brother's football games or to the beach all the time. We were a team.

My parents also supported my dreams. They let me start modeling at an incredibly young age, and about the age of 12 or 13, as I became passionate about modeling, I remember my parents came up with the money for me to go to the John Casablancas school of Modeling. It was something that they encouraged me to do, and I still love being in front of a camera or walking the catwalk on a runway.

I am proud that my husband and I work together as an effective team. We are both busy entrepreneurs, but our family comes first. Not only do we make sure we are at sporting events and extracurriculars, we never forget a birthday or important holiday. We enjoy spending time and celebrating our children. When our girls were younger, my husband would take flowers and candy to their school for Valentine's Day. Even though they are older, he still showers them with gifts and love. Not to leave my sons out, I have always made sure that I give them a gift and they never turn down candy from Mom.

Another family tradition is to celebrate Christmas at my mother-in-law, Donna's house. She prepares her annual seafood dinner. The table is set with a mountain of food for everyone, including salmon, shrimp, and crab legs . . . lots of crab legs. Of course, we have the regular items such as vegetables, turkey, rice, collard greens, and yams. After our tummies are full, we exchange gifts and dance the night away. Did I mention the delicious desserts? My mother-in-law prepares all the desserts herself, from scratch. No pre-made, store bought nonsense is allowed in her house. The desserts are plentiful and scrumptious. The house is filled with laughter and love. We've been doing this tradition for over eighteen years.

The fun doesn't stop there. We wake up the next morning and travel to Sanford, North Carolina where my husband is from to visit his family. Then we stop over to my father-in-law's home in Sanford. For years, my father-in-law Fred and his wife Gaynelle would welcome us into their home for the Christmas holiday and we would always have a memorable time.

As you can guess, Thanksgiving is a big production in our family also. We have more people at Thanksgiving than the Macy's parade! Well, almost. The house is filled with my mom, dad, sister, brother, their families, and then extended families. I love to cook, and my collard greens are always a hit. Our children love my food, and it makes me feel good to know they enjoy eating their momma's soul food, especially since they know their daddy runs a soul food restaurant. They know I cook it with love.

I am proud of our children. They are all wonderful, intelligent, talented individuals. No two are alike, and I wouldn't have it any other way.

Brianna and Kalie are our twin daughters. They're the oldest of our seven children and have grown into beautiful confident young women, who have given us beautiful, confident grandchildren. Like most twins, when they were little, they did everything together. Somewhere around sixth grade, they started to develop more individual interests.

Our oldest son, Nicholas, is the go-getter in the family. He is always on the grind to make things happen. My birthday and his are just one day a part, so the celebration rocks the city. He's my Leo twin.

Jasmine Savon Mary Kay is the middle child, three on both sides of her (three older and three younger). She's one of our college students and a future veterinarian. Her middle name is Mary Kay. I named her Mary Kay, and most people think it's because of my Mary Kay business; however, she's named after both of her grandmothers. My mom's name is Mary, and my mother-in-law's name is Kay. When she was younger, this girl went everywhere with me; her nickname "GoGo" since she was always on the go. Jasmine is the child I never had to worry about, parenting her came easy. She is so creative and loves to craft and work with her hands, I believe she gets that from my father. I admire her

6

passion for knowledge she never had to be forced to go to school. When she was younger, she would wake up every day and get dressed, pack her book bag with the older kids, and wait at the bus stop with them. The gag was she wasn't even old enough to go to school yet! In high school she played volleyball, softball, golf, and she swam. She was awarded female athlete of the year, she's so talented and driven. Furthermore, she graduated high school in the top 10% of her class. Still striving for excellence in college, Jasmine was a freshman senator, president of her dorm, has studied abroad and has been on the Dean's list every semester in college. I love to see the way her mind works. My other children joke that she is the golden child. I just praise God that she has grown into a beautiful successful woman.

Jaylen is my bookworm. He's my most intellectual child. He's very humble and he has never disrespected any adult. He's a brainiac; I call him that because he can fix anything that has to do with the computer or electronics. He knows all about computer programming. When he was three, he called himself a baby genius, and he's carried that title in our family. He developed a love for reading books, and he'd ask me to buy him books from the bookstore that would be over 1000 pages and he would read all of them in two to three days! He's a computer science engineer and he's going to be incredibly successful. He hates working with his hands, but he loves working with his brain.

Jevon Jr. is my outgoing child. He's very charismatic, charming and the most athletic. He loves football and he's passionate about helping people. He loves his family and he's the loudest one in our home. When he's away from home, the house is quiet. His goal is to make it to the National Football League, but he also loves science and his strong plan B is to become a scientist. He often tells me how he's going to buy me three houses and hire a personal chef because we both love exotic cuisines. He has so much determination, focus and this young man has a lot of heart... he has the heart of a lion!

Jade is the baby of the family. She is literally number seven which stands for God's divine number and it stands for completion. She completes us! She is beautiful, outgoing, fun-loving, athletic, passionate about hair, and the left chamber of my heart. She's a beautiful soul & spirit. Ever since she was little, she dreamed of becoming a pediatrician and now is interested in Law Enforcement because she wants to make our country better. I love how much she loves expanding her horizon and trying out new things, I honestly see a lot of myself in her. She is baby number seven, the LAST of this batch of the Mcivers.

As parents, my husband and I have worked hard to give our children the proper guidance and nurturing in life. As they go out into the world, we can only hope they will rely on the principles we've given them. As parents, we may not agree with all of their choices and decisions, but we will never stop loving them. Jevon and I couldn't be prouder of our children and their achievements in life. We look forward to seeing even greater things from them. One of my favorite scriptures is 1 Corinthians 13: 7; *Love bears all things, believes all things, hopes all things, and endures all things.*

My husband is my partner in life, and he is an amazing role model for our children. He shows them a strong work ethic; demonstrating you can achieve your goals in life. United, we show our children a strong commitment to marriage - and life's challenges? We face them together.

In our marriage, we enjoy and respect each other. We still take long walks in the park. We share our hopes, dreams, and fears. We tackle the hard subjects, and we love each other through them. With God as our source of strength, it keeps us centered and humbled to concentrate on our family. I love us!

#Tishtalk

Who is your family? Sometimes family happens due to blood ... or marriage ... or just bonds of care. Write out your family. Talk about what they give to you, how they help you, and what you do for them in return. Thank our most loving God for providing such a wonderful family.

_____

_____

_____

_____

_____

_____

_____

_____

_____

_____

_____

_____

_____

_____

_____

_____

_____

_____

_____

_____

_____

_____

_____

_____

_____

_____

_____

_____

_____

_____

_____

_____

2

THE G WORD

I AM BLESSED with some amazing girlfriends. We share the good, the bad, and the ugly. We have adventures and dynamic travel. These ladies are my ride or die, and our friendships are forever. Every girlfriend has a role. Who are your girlfriends that you are doing life with? We will explore the distinct types of girlfriends and why they are important.

Not only do I have an amazing family, I have been blessed with some amazing friends. I have a wide circle of associates and acquaintances, but I have a dynamic group of ladies who are my "ride or die girls." These particular friendships have been going for twenty or more years. All from different walks of life and spread throughout the country, the world in fact. They are my girlfriends and there is nothing better than having girlfriend power to encourage, lift, strengthen, motivate, and sustain me. These ladies are diverse in what they each bring to my life. Together they are the perfect blend of friendship.

Do you have the right blend of friends? Not every girlfriend can meet every need. However, just the right mix can give you a well-rounded, close circle of friends who can be there for the good and bad times. Studies show, your relationship with your girlfriends can potentially outlast your marriage and your coworkers.

I feel there is a blueprint for great friendship. Many qualities we look for in our friends are the same ones we possess. Do you agree? Make a list of all the qualities and standards you require to have a healthy relationship or friendship.

Remember that successful friendships require both individuals to be inside of the 'ship' together, but if one person jumps ship or abandons the 'ship', the other may feel isolated. It is not about spending money because like my mother says, you can't buy friends. You must invest and spend time to foster and nurture the relationship or sisterhood. It's important to define boundaries with friends. You don't ever want to isolate yourself from a dependable, loyal friend. With friends you can talk about anything from age to family, religion, and careers. With friends, you can keep secrets that you share amongst each other. You can talk about the past, former or current lovers. You should not have over dependency or toxicity in friendship.

Here are the girlfriends every queen should have:

The Relationship Girlfriend. Genuinely wants to see you happy but does not want to see you hurt in the romance department. She offers sound advice and is not negative or bitter. She listens with a listening ear. She is not a "man-hater" but is a "man-helper." She is a sucker for love. She will be your "wing person" when you are looking for a man, your advice central when you are in a relationship, and should the worst happen and you break up with your love, she's the first one at your door with wine and ice cream.

The Business Girlfriend. She cares about your career or business aspirations. You both have things in common about business goals. She encourages you and you encourage her to be the best. You can bounce an idea off her and she will not share it. If anything, she will dig in to take it from idea to reality. She is not a mentor. You are two equals, propelling each other to manifest your dreams.

The Fun Girlfriend. She is the one you call when you want to have a good time, no holds barred. Whether you are hitting the town or sitting by the fire, watching your favorite movie, you can always count on her for a good laugh and a really good time.

The Wise Girlfriend. You can count on her to tell you like it is. If something is stupid, she tells you. She does it with love and forces you to see the ramifications. She is the girlfriend who says, "Slow your roll. Are you sure, you want to do this?"

The Good Mom Girlfriend. She is the friend you consider to be an excellent mother. You can call on her for advice from anything to little Johnny is running a fever to ideas for your daughter's sweet sixteenth birthday party. She helps you stay grounded and sane as a mom.

The Event Planning Girlfriend. This is the girlfriend that helps you plan any event, from parties to anniversaries. She is the girlfriend who can design on a budget and the end result is stellar. She is meticulous and knows what will represent you well. She asks for no credit because she genuinely enjoys helping her friends.

The Praying Girlfriend. This is the girlfriend who does not mind dropping everything to offer you a word of prayer. She is the one who says, "Girl, let's pray about this situation." My friends have told me that I am this girlfriend. I genuinely believe a family that prays together, stays together. My girlfriends are included as a part of my family. James 5:16 says the effectual fervent prayer of a righteous man availeth much.

The Travel Girlfriend. This is the girlfriend that will literally have a bag packed and in front of your house in thirty minutes or less at the mere mention of a vacay or road trip. No one knows how she manages to get out of work, but she is your go-to when you need a getaway. She is adaptable and ready for adventure.

Do you have girlfriends who fit these categories? Are there any missing categories? My girlfriends have told me that I fit all of these. I think this is why my phone stays active with calls, texts, and posts to my social media accounts.

#Tishtalk

Name your girlfriends and the categories they fit. If you are missing any girlfriends, go out today and find someone who fits the description. Like I've said before, we all need our girlfriends, so keep them close.

_____
_____
_____
_____
_____
_____
_____
_____
_____
_____
_____
_____
_____
_____
_____
_____
_____
_____
_____
_____
_____
_____
_____
_____
_____
_____
_____
_____
_____
_____

3

FACE THE MIRROR

WHO AM I? I am Lakertisha Slade Mciver. Tish to most people. Wife, mother, daughter, sister, friend, business mogul, community leader, church activist ... I am so many things. I am not perfect, but I have an undeniable quest to be my perfect self. This is what motivates me. When I find that I don't like my current situation, I start a path to change it. While change doesn't happen overnight, it does start with you and only you, no one can make the change for you. Sure, you can be guided or given tips and tools, but true change starts with you. My advice is to face the mirror. What do I mean? Face your situation and make peace with it. You can't walk away if you don't know where you're going.

I know it's not easy. It's not a simple situation.

When I was the girl locked in the shack with a crazy man, I was the one who put together a plan. I was the one who popped open the window and ran for my life. It wasn't like there was anyone else who could do it for me.

Bad stuff happens. My life isn't perfect. It isn't always smooth sailing. It ebbs and flows. It goes up and down. You either, hold on and plan to rise, or drown when you're at the bottom. There's no way for you to go up if you are clinging to the bottom.

Several years ago, I remember a time when I was vulnerable and felt like things were beyond my control. It was during the time our family restaurant business had a fire. It wasn't a small fire, and my husband Jevon was severely burned. I was worried about his health, his well-being and how we were going to make it financially.

Jevon was and still is my knight in shining armor. Every day, he worked tirelessly at the restaurant. He and his mother Donna, as owners they did whatever it took to make the restaurant successful. This man would work the register, cook, maintain inventory, manage the staff, and balance the books. One of the main things that attracted me to him, besides his handsome looks, was his amazing brain for business. Not only is he a successful entrepreneur, but he's a heck of an accountant also. He's my number cruncher. His mom taught him about numbers as a young man she said he loved math. I think it has to be a natural gift from God that he possesses because me, on the other hand, I don't like numbers so much except making and counting my money. I'm so glad that I married an accountant; because those are the two classes I struggled with in college, Cost Accounting and Managerial Accounting. I always knew that I would hire an accountant, but God allowed me to marry one.

On one Sunday afternoon, I was leaving church and I was craving some soul food. I didn't want to cook at home and Jevon would always tell me to stop by, to get food to feed the kids and me. So, this particular Sunday it was strange and different, I drove by and saw fire trucks and an ambulance in the parking lot and immediately got concerned. I pulled up and a few employees ran out the building and said that my husband, the one I counted on every day to be our provider, was burned in a fire.

This hurt because I didn't know what to expect as I followed the ambulance to the hospital. All I knew was Jevon was severely burned. The children were a little afraid of him because the skin was burned off his face and hands. I think the biggest part for them was seeing their big, strong father so physically weak. For me, for the first time in our relationship, I had to be strong for Jevon, the kids and myself. I had to keep us afloat.

At first, my prayers were me screaming, "Why God??" Then I heard God say, *I need your attention. I need you to humble yourself before me. I will keep you in perfect peace.*

Every day, I would get up and pray:

Father God, cover my husband and pains. Give him strength to endure. He is your child. Lord, I am crying out to you to for help. I know that no weapon formed against me shall Prosper. Help my children not be afraid of their father due to this temporary condition. Help me not be afraid of how we are going to make it.

This was a process, a humbling process, with almost brutal intensity. I didn't want to leave him, but I had to go out and make money for us. No, we weren't broke and yes, there were savings, but that was a last resort. Reluctantly, I would leave Jevon in the capable hands of his nurses—hands that weren't mine. I would go out and work my Mary Kay business.

My strategy was to hold three appointments a day while he was in the hospital and the nurses were taking care of him. I would take the night shift, nursing my husband back to health, cooking, cleaning, doing homework with the kids, and running my Mary Kay unit. That was the routine. I would get up each day ready to work my business.

My day started at dark thirty. Not 5:30 am, but dark thirty. I would wake up, pray, cook breakfast, get the kids ready for school and get Jevon ready for a day with his nurses. Then all of a sudden, I became the only nurse, and this is when I had to increase my prayer life and meditation just to keep thing balanced. Being a caretaker for my spouse was new to me but if felt so natural because I was a mom already. However it is a little different for your partner, because although you use the same nurturing trait that you use as mothers, and the same compassion and love, it's different . . . because it is a fine line with a Man that has Pride.

Many women want to know my secret sauce; how to balance raising children, while taking care of the home, making it work. It's not really about balancing as much as it is about centering. YOU MUST FIND YOUR CENTER! God was my center then and now.

16

Wow! I remember those mornings were busy and hectic, but as God promised, he kept me in perfect peace. Yes, there were days I was physically tired but never spiritually. I'm a morning person and I looked forward to the quiet of the early day; it was my prayer time with God. I would pour out my heart to Him. Afterwards, I would feel energized. I was eating, sleeping, breathing, and walking in His word. The joy of the Lord was my strength. My smile never left my face. It wasn't a fake smile either. You know the one, when people ask sometimes sincerely and sometimes a little nosily, "How is everything? How are *you* holding up?" I would answer with a genuine smile, "Excellent. Thanks for asking."

It was one of the most difficult times I have ever experienced as a married woman, but I learned so much in the process. I learned how strong I was, and the strength of our relationship. Not only did we learn about the strength of our relationship with each other, but our relationship with God. We relied on Him. Our family worked together, everyone pulling their weight. We were the mighty Mcivers. This was truly the beginning of our slogan #MciverStrong

My attitude shows itself in everything I do. My attitude is so powerful that people can sense it before I say a word. On social media, most of my followers always notice that I am smiling and genuinely look happy. Why? I *am* happy! My attitude determines both my simplest and complicated actions—from the way I carry myself to the way I deal with hard times.

Let me be clear, attitude is changeable. As attitude changes, so do feelings. I, too, have my down days. I will admit they're not often, but I do have them.

While I was celebrating my big four-oh in Florida, my mom received a phone call telling us that my maternal grandparents were killed in a house fire. My mom was with me and my family, helping to celebrate my birthday when we received the devastating news. We had spent the day enjoying the sun, laughing, and loving as only we can do when celebrating. Who could have imagined that one late-night phone call would change our world forever? My grandparents, both gone. My mom's parents. I hugged my mom like I never hugged her before. How did this happen? Is this for real? It felt like a dream. Immediately, we traveled back to Charlotte.

They say when it rains, it pours. Not only did my grandparents die in a house fire, there was suspicion of foul play. In the days that followed, we had to deal with police and media. As a family, we dealt with all of this as we mourned and planned a double funeral. It was hard to say goodbye to my grandparents. It was also hard to watch my children say goodbye to their great-grandparents. Most of all, it was heart-wrenching to watch my mom and her siblings say goodbye to their parents.

Through it all, my mom was a rock. I looked at her strength, knowing she was grieving, and admired her attitude. She relied on her family and her faith to move forward. In my family, our faith is our foundation. My mom is and has always been the ultimate example for me. She didn't fall apart. She was steadfast, unmovable. She handled her business. After all, she came from a long line of strong women. Mary Slade taught me how to view myself. She taught me to love myself, and for that, I am forever grateful.

There have been so many times I've been knocked down by life. So many challenges that have thrown me for a loop and each time I have felt like I was down for the count. And yet, I always find a way to stand back up again. I've done this enough times that I learned to become my best motivator. Now, I think I embrace challenges and thrive to find ways to forge ahead.

Look at what's happened to you. Is holding onto that memory helping you? Is being the person knocked off their feet giving anything to you or is it taking everything away? You have to decide to act for you. You have to see that you aren't the bad things that happen. You are the person who rises. Who would you rather be ... the victim or the victor? I remember sitting on that airplane coming back from Jamaica after being kidnapped and held for hours fighting for my life, I decided right then and there that I would rise like a phoenix and no one would have that much power over me. What I'm saying is *take your power back*, You OWN IT!

Psychiatry and therapy are great, but they don't work for everyone. Not everyone can sit and talk about their problems to a stranger. Some of us don't have the mental construction to handle that kind of introspection. Some people just need to put what happened behind them and move on. They just need to acknowledge it.

There have been setbacks in my life. I've dealt with disappointments, breakups, betrayals, and death of family and friends. I'm sure you've had the same in life. Do you not like where you are? Do you not like the quality … or lack of quality … in your life? Do you long for bigger things? Do you want more? Are you tired of looking in the mirror and not seeing what you envisioned? Are you tired of looking in your loved ones' eyes and not seeing a success? Or someone to be admired?

Well, change. It's just that simple. Identify what you don't like and transform into what you do like. Put aside those stale and ancient beliefs that this is all you are and choose differently.

If you went to a restaurant and ordered a steak … and the waitress brought you a burger … would you just accept it? Are you really going to just eat that burger, secretly longing for that juicy steak? Of course not. You are going to point out to the waitress that she got it wrong, and she needs to fix it. You would never pay for a steak and eat the burger instead. Well, guess what? You pay for the choices you accept in this journey with your life. Why would you possibly settle for less?

Only you can tell the universe what you want. Only you can revise your order and get something new. The power is and will always be in your hands.

#Tishtalk

What's your situation? What do you want to change? Write it down. Words have power. God created an entire universe when he uttered a single word. So, write it down. Make it real. What do you need to face and/or move on from? What's your "thing" that you want to happen? What new order do you want the universe to know?

_____

_____

_____

_____

_____

_____

_____

_____

_____

_____

_____

_____

_____

_____

_____

_____

_____

_____

_____

_____

_____

_____

_____

_____

_____

_____

4

START WITH THE RIGHT FACE

DID I mention that after you face your situation, the next step is to do something about it? The first place you can start, when you wish to change that order, is by changing the person you see when you look in the mirror.

I was at an event recently, and there were several women who asked me how to change their professional image. Some wanted to know how to change it for their personal lives too. One of my great joys is helping women become their best self. It is my true passion.

Empowering people is definitely at the top of my priority list. When you can change the way people view themselves, then you can change your community, then the nation, and ultimately the world. What's your signature feature? Mine is my smile. Don't laugh, I am very proud of that smile. In my business, I smile a lot. It's a part of my brand ... I want to make a huge impact in the world, and that impact starts with my smile!

Have you seen a woman that looks like she is gliding instead of walking? Who shines so brightly you can feel it even before she walks into a room? No doubt her presence is accentuated by her clothes, shoes, hair, and jewelry. Her nails are done, makeup perfect, her outfit looks pristine and never wrinkled or dirty. In short, she is what we call "together."

Every woman should know her style and learn how to maximize it at every opportunity. I'm a seasoned entrepreneur, and I know that my style is a part of my image. Every morning, I get dressed for the "unplanned" meeting. I don't wake up to be mediocre. I wake up to win … in business and in love. I want to make sure that my husband spends his day looking forward to coming home to me. I want every person who sees me to think, "I have got to get into business with her." This is the attitude I have as soon as my eyelids flicker as I start to wake up. The moment my stilettos hit the pavement; I am ready for anything.

My fashion sense is truly genetic. My parents were both fashion-forward and very stylish. I would see them get dressed up to go out, and they would be looking good and smelling good.

My father, Herman "NIP" Slade, would walk into a room and light the whole room up with his smile. He was the happiest and strongest man in my life. He loved his family and taught me the value of family. I remember going to family reunions in Mount Holly, North Carolina, to bond and learn family history. I have so many great memories with my dad – long phone conversations, with him encouraging me to be my best, and watching football games together. My love of sports definitely came from my dad.

My dad was the definition of smooth. The man could dress! Everything he wore looked like it was made for him. He taught me how to coordinate and accessorize my outfits. He taught me how make sure all eyes are always on me. I used to love watching my parents get ready for a night on the town. The getting ready was just as epic as their arrival to their event. When my dad passed away, I vowed to pass down his legacy of wisdom and keen fashion sense to our children and grandchildren.

I've been told that I have the "It" factor. It's what the French call je ne sais quoi. It's literally an unexplainable quality. You either have it or you don't. Me? I was born with it. When I walk into a room, I automatically turn heads. It's not just my hair, my clothes, my shoes, or my makeup. It's the way that I put all these elements together that makes it undeniable hard for anyone to ignore. Even if they don't want to, they can't help but to look. The family joke is that when I enter a room, "I don't turn heads, I break necks!" That's je ne sais quoi.

My mother, Mary Hill Slade, is the most straightforward, honest, humorous, and amazing woman I know. She's very family oriented and loves her children and grandchildren. She's passionate about helping people. I recall during my childhood, my mom would feed the whole neighborhood. She was the community mom. She loves her family and her friends. I definitely get that from my mom. I am loyal to my friends, and I love to cook. I grew up watching my mom cook for everybody. She's known for her sweet potato pie, potato salad, and golden fried fish and chicken wings. Not only can I cook like my mom, I inherited her love for travel. Growing up, I watched her go on trips and vowed I would do the same.

In addition to my parents, there were so many people who helped shaped me into the woman that I am today. My mom's oldest sister, Aunt Phyllis, whom I called my PhD because her initials matched her intellect, was my ultimate cheerleader. She believed in my dreams and would breathe life into my goals and ambitions. When she passed away, it was the one of the hardest things I've had to endure. In addition to Aunt Phyllis and my dad, I've had four other people to pass away who were monumental in my life: Ronnell Gardner (my ex-boyfriend from high school), Chris Chavis (my ex-boyfriend from college), Aunt Mary Ann Slade, and Bessie President (my paternal grandmother). My point is the people in your life can help shape who you are and who you become. However, it is up to you to take action and define your life.

If you are interested in staying ahead of the game, you must make sure you are reflecting the right image. I often say, "Image is everything", and "When You Look Good, You Feel Good!" If you want people to take you seriously your image must be Tight! Dress for where you are going, not for where you are and the last time I checked, you need to want to do business with YOU. I often train my team the value in this and you must do a "Check Up from the Neck Up". Is your lipstick in place, is your hair tight and if not, get it right...just ask your self – would you want to conduct business with you?? I always knew that I wanted to hire a professional stylist and I did when I could afford one. I love her and she's still a part of my team (my image team), I refer to them as my GLAM SQUAD... Dream Team. DO you have a GLAM SQUAD?? If you don't, we live in a world of technology, Facetime one of your fashionista girlfriends before you arrive at the party and see if your outfit is SLAMMIN'... Make sure you get your own outfits coordinated if you cannot afford to hire someone. Are you a head turner or are heads turning away?

Do you have the WOW Factor?

☑ Amazing HAIR

☑ Perfect BROWS and LASHES

☑ Fab MANI / PEDI

☑ Fierce JEWELS

☑ Stylish OUTFIT

☑ On-Point SHOE GAME

☑ Great FRAGRANCE

Amazing hair. Short, long, perm, weave, sew-in, or texturizer. Hair is an extension of personality. Choose a style that fits you and one that you can maintain. If you rock a short style, keep it shaped up. New growth is inevitable, slick down those edges! For shoulder length hair and beyond, don't settle for traditional. Create bouncy, bold curls. Wave it up. Up-dos are not just for proms anymore. Put the "P" in Ponytail by making it a high pony, one that will get noticed. Work your weave. Buy quality hair and see a professional stylist. Spice it up with color-purples, pinks, and reds are always hot colors but no color is off limit. The possibilities are endless.

Perfect brows and lashes. First things first, don't do them yourself. Your eyebrows and lashes define your face. One wrong move, you could go from a friendly face to an angry betty. For lashes, you can play with length. It all depends on the occasion. For date night (and yes, married people should have date night, it's actually more important for them than it is for single ladies), put on a longer lash. Chances are someone will be gazing longingly into your eyes.

Fab Mani/Pedi. Long or short, your nails should be fabulous. Like most things, you can glam them up or down, but they must be clean, neat, and ready to shine. A weekly manicure and pedicure are key. If you live in a big city you may want to get that manicure done more than once a week. To achieve strong healthy nails, protein is the answer. Eat lean poultry, beef, and fish. Don't forget the veggies. Spinach is a good source of protein. Remember to keep your nails moisturized. Make it a habit to put on hand cream every time you wash them.

Fierce jewelry. My biggest pet peeve is to lose one of my earrings. All my earrings are fierce because I make sure of it. I love earrings. I feel naked without them, so much so, that I keep a pair or two in my car that can almost go with anything. I always wear jewelry that will become a conversation starter. Wear unique bracelets, necklaces, and rings. I love big, bold, shiny jewelry. In my line of business, I make sure my jewelry is designed to "attract and not attack."

Stylish outfit. I never have a "plain" day, or what others may call a "dress down day." Dress down for what? I'm never in jeans and a t-shirt. If I am, it's my most flattering and embellished with rhinestones or a dramatic pair of jeans enhanced by some stilettos and t-shirt with a little bling. To be honest, I really don't own any jeans because I hate to wear them. I think blue jeans are a bit boring and subpar in the scheme of things. Now I am not trying to cause any controversy, but I think women should put a little bit more effort into their look. I learned this in my business of Mary Kay, women feel more powerful in a skirt or a dress! We are empowered and walk with more "pep in our step."

I like to say, "When you look good ... you feel good." This is my mantra, or my motto, if you prefer. My family and friends will tell you I always show up in a skirt, power suit, or it's going to be a beautiful dress with killer heels. The more fabulous it is, the better. Men can put on jeans. They wear slacks and pants all day long and believe me, they're comfortable, but they cannot put on a killer skirt with killer legs, paired with some killer snakeskin pumps and grab attention like a woman. YASSSSSS!!! Okay, so I'm over-the-top, and I like to be stylish. It is who I am. I'm not conservative at all - so, the more "bling" the better. I love sequins and shiny things. I guess you can call me flashy! Your clothes say a lot about you. Don't believe me? Go to the mall and sit for five minutes. You will judge a few people without even wanting to judge them. Your outfit doesn't have to have designer tags to be stylish. Jazz it up with some signature pieces—statement pieces of jewelry, scarves, belts and sunglasses are a must. Don't forget to rock an amazing handbag, clutch, or even a cute wristlet. Find that accessory that takes you straight to fabulous!

On point shoe game. I love shoes. I love shoes. Did I tell you that I love shoes? To be clear, I love SEXY shoes. You know the ones. The shoes that give you that extra sway in your walk when entering the boardroom or the bedroom. Peak-a-boos, open toes, sling backs, lattices. Heels or not? Heels. Six inches to be exact, taller if you can handle it. You will look slimmer, taller, and, most important of all, sexy.

Great fragrance. Whenever someone says my perfume smells good that makes me feel good, too. We all know body chemistry is essential to a great smelling fragrance. What smells good on me may not smell good on you. Find the fragrance that is the perfect blend of you: citrus, floral, aquatic, fruity, or spicy. Are you sexy, bold, sweet, strong, daring, or innocent? What statement are you trying to make? Your fragrance should match that. I love to get on an elevator with people and they start to look around like "who has on that beautiful fragrance," I then immediately look up and say you like that smell, it's so and so ... whatever the designer fragrance I have on at the time. My point is that a great scent can be sexy like a great outfit. My husband tells me all the time that he loves the way that I smell. He said that is one of the major things that attracted him to me was my scent! Yes, ladies we have a scent. I'm not talking about the old-school terminology of pheromones that people talked about back in the day. Invest in some great smelling perfume and walk on the runway of life with your head held high.

You can start out slow. Look at your lips, one of the most important features on a woman's face. A man is more drawn to a woman's lips that any other facial feature, according to research by Manchester University. It's been said that the redder the lipstick the longer the look. While lipsticks come in all colors and shades, the goal is to find the shades most flattering to you. Let's face it; putting on your favorite lipstick can make you feel like a new woman.

It is rare that I leave the house without lipstick. If I am running to the store, I put it on. I definitely wear my lipstick when attending meetings at my kids' schools and even quick runs to the mall. I call it "putting my face on." I even wear lipstick to the beach! The sun's a harsh mistress, I want to look good.

I know it sounds like a vanity move, but there is power in lipstick. Lipstick makes you look younger, look more attractive, and you feel confident and ready for anything.

As we get older, our skin tone darkens and adding a pop of color to your lips brings a flattering contrast. In addition, the color red has always been associated with power. For women, a power suit is usually red. Studies have shown that the same goes for red lips. Women wearing red lipstick feel more confident and empowered. The color red is a magnet. Try it. Put on some red lipstick and notice how others treat you. In fact, wearing red lipsticks can make you feel more confident about your day. Whether the goal is to impact others or yourself, a little bit of lipstick goes a long way. Does your significant other greet you with a more attentive smile? If you don't have a trusty shade of red lipstick in your bag, I advise you to place an order with the closest Mary Kay consultant.

#Tishtalk

Look in the mirror. The better your outside looks, the better your inside will feel. Start from the top of your head and keep going until you hit your toes. Change. Dress up. Rebuke the modern attitude of t-shirts and jeans. Dress like you're going to Church or even to a formal event. I don't care if you're just running to the store for a gallon of milk. Ever hear the saying, "Dress for the job you want, not the one you have?" I say, "Dress for the LIFE you want, not the one you have." You'd be amazed at how empowering it can be, and once you are empowered, magical things can happen.

_____
_____
_____
_____
_____
_____
_____
_____
_____
_____
_____
_____
_____
_____
_____
_____
_____
_____
_____
_____
_____
_____

5

CREATE GOOD HABITS

I'VE HEARD it said that a habit takes twenty-one days to form. I'm not sure how true this is, but I do know that you must repeatedly do something to make it a habit. Did I just state the obvious? Yes. By some accounts, it's said that it could take two weeks to 6 months to break a habit, especially one that you've spent so long to develop. The truth is breaking a habit means establishing a new habit.

The time it takes to break a habit depends on three factors. First, is there a new habit to take its place? Second, do you want to break the habit? Third, are you physically and mentally able to break the habit? Breaking a habit means you break the connection it provides between you and the behavior.

I strive to be habitually positive. Of course, I'm no Pollyanna, but I do try to see the positive in any situation. If I don't see the positive, I use it as a learning opportunity. I always see the glass as half full, never half empty. Yep, that's me, "Mrs. Optimistic". With so much tragedy and despair in today's world, it is extremely easy to become cynical and negative. I have found a few ways to help combat that and remain positive.

• • •

1. Keep a gratitude journal.

With the busy hustle of the day to day, sometimes the bad things outweigh the good things. We tend to remember the bad things: I missed my train, my heel broke, I was late for my meeting, and my son forgot his track spikes and I was super mom and beat traffic to get them to him in time. However, we need to cling to the good parts of the day: I missed my train but had a great conversation with a kind lady, my heel broke but my feet felt so much better in flats, my meeting would have been too long anyways, having my son sincerely thank me for helping him start his race on time was worth it. Get the idea? Try writing down 5 things that you feel grateful for every day and see how your attitude changes.

2. Use Positive Words.

I am constantly reminding my children that words have power. I know it sounds cliché, but it's true. What you say about your life, is how your life will be. Perception starts with you. If you feel your life is boring and stagnant, so will others. If you feel your life is electric and exciting, so will others. The key is to enjoy your life. If you can't describe your life as enjoyable, then it simply won't be. A person who enjoys their life, usually smiles a lot. There is no secret that I enjoy my life to the fullest.

3. Don't fall into the complaint trap.

Often, our day is going pretty well until we encounter other people and take on their complaint or issue. One of my favorite stories from Elite Executive National Sales Director, Gloria Mayfield Banks, in Mary Kay is that she found herself saying she was tired every day when she worked in Corporate America. Until one day, it hit her. She wasn't tired. She was just saying what others were saying because she had fallen into the complaint trap. You'll find that people complain less without the validation of others.

4. Be a problem solver.

Being positive doesn't mean that you must be oblivious to problems. If you're going to point out problems in people or situations, place just as much effort into suggesting solutions. I detest people who immediately point out the problem and offer no solution. What's worse is this person usually keeps repeating the problem over and over again (yes, insert eye roll). My team knows that a pet peeve. If you're not willing to roll up your sleeves and problem solve, you may as well leave. Even if you can't solve the problem, you should at least offer ways to make it better.

5. Make someone else smile.

I'm always complimenting my friends, family, and even strangers. It's important to give a sincere compliment. Wouldn't it be a much better world if we focused on the good and not the bad? If you work hard enough, you can find something nice to say about anyone. I know there are some real "challenges" living amongst us, but I truly feel that God has a purpose for us all. Truthfully, most of the time, I don't have to say anything, I simply smile. Even if the person doesn't smile back, they usually reciprocate in some manner –a held door, extra whip cream or an upgrade.

Tishtalk

What five things are you most grateful?

_____

_____

_____

_____

_____

_____

_____

_____

_____

_____

_____

_____

_____

_____

_____

_____

_____

_____

_____

_____

_____

_____

_____

_____

_____

_____

_____

6

DATE NIGHT

THERE IS one habit that my husband and I have continued since being married – date night! Once a week, we go out on a date. This means no kids or any other adults. It's considered our alone time. We look forward to this time because with a large family like ours, we stay on the go with the kids. Our date night activities are varied: dinner, movies, driving to the next city or flying to a remote location like the Virgin Islands. That's his favorite. In all the years we've been married, there has never been a dull date night. We keep it spicy!

Tips for a successful date night:

- Do not, I repeat, do not bring any extra people. Just you and your mate.
- Think about fulfilling a fantasy that you or your mate may have. Listen to your favorite song while riding in the car to get you in the mood.
- Hire a babysitter that can spend the night just in case you get

lucky. The sitter must be flexible while you are out with your boo thang on date night because you may not make it home!

- Make reservations early to your favorite restaurant. Did you know that dinner and a movie are foreplay on date night?
- Be spontaneous. Switch it up so that you or your spouse (or significant other) have a chance to plan the actual "date night."
- Intimacy plays a major role in any relationship, so make sure you enjoy each other's company. Recline those seats in the SUV and have fun.
- Finally, remind your special someone how much you love and appreciate them and their time. Go ahead and schedule the next date night just like you would at any business meeting. Only this time, it's business and pleasure!

#Tishtalk

How do you make your date nights successful?

_____

_____

_____

_____

_____

_____

_____

_____

_____

_____

_____

_____

_____

_____

_____

_____

_____

_____

_____

_____

_____

_____

_____

_____

_____

_____

_____

_____

#Tishtalk

What are your favorite places to have a romantic dinner?

_____

_____

_____

_____

_____

_____

_____

_____

_____

_____

_____

_____

_____

_____

_____

_____

_____

_____

_____

_____

_____

_____

_____

_____

_____

#Tishtalk

List a few date night songs that you both enjoy.

_____
_____
_____
_____
_____
_____
_____
_____
_____
_____
_____
_____
_____
_____
_____
_____
_____
_____
_____
_____
_____
_____
_____
_____
_____
_____

7

DRIVE OUT DRAMA

No More Drama! ... Do you remember that song? I loved that jam! Mary J. Blige's fifth studio album became the rallying cry for most women who were dealing with relationship issues. The inspiration for the album came largely from Blige's own self-destructive life stemming from drug and alcohol abuse. In addition, she was involved in a series of abusive relationships. In short, she was tired of the drama.

As the woman of the house, I honestly believe that women set the pace for their households. Of course, I strongly believe men have a definitive role as well, but let's focus on the role of the lady of the house. As the woman of the house, you encourage and nurture. Your words ring in your little one's ears throughout their day at school and play. Your words of support and comfort give your husband the strength and courage to keep reaching for his goals. If everyone is focused on positive goals, it leaves little room for negativity and drama. In short, words matter.

Here are some tips to keep your household, and life, drama free:

1. Speak positive words.

2. Stop making excuses.
3. Speak it into existence.
4. Encourage yourself.

Speak Positive Words

What words do you use daily? Do you use positive words even in the face of a challenge? There is power in words. A simple word or phrase can alter your mood from happy to sad. Look at the words and terms below and notice your emotion when reading each one.

Brilliant
Stupid
Yes!
No!
Happy to report
Regret to inform you
Clean
Dirty
Singing your praises
Giving you an earful
Fresh
Foul
Beautiful
Ugly
Wonderful
Horrible
Well done
You suck
Way to go
What did you do

Take notice of the words and phrases you use daily. Start to replace the negative ones with positive and notice the difference it makes in your environment.

Stop Making Excuses

When I was younger, I remember the phrase; excuses are like noses and everyone has one. As an adult, I have heard many versions of this, but let's stick to this one. My point is, that no one likes excuses or a sad story. Sad stories are like the appetizer for drama. Don't get me wrong, there is nothing wrong with venting or talking about something bad that happened to you. Just don't talk about it over and over again. Don't let your needle get stuck. Remember when I said you have to tell the universe you have the wrong order and you're not willing to settle? Well, in that situation, in a restaurant, you wouldn't keep telling the waitress over and over again you want to change your order. You wouldn't keep talking about how you got the wrong thing … or at least you wouldn't if you don't want to be seen as a jerk. As the wife of a restaurateur, believe me, I know. When you continue to talk about negative events, you are pulled right back into the emotion and heartache of it all. It's like scar tissue, the wound has healed, but the scar is still there. Don't let others take you back to that space either.

Speak it into Existence

Or at least, create an image so you can see your future. One of the things that I enjoy with my family is creating vision boards. We enjoy setting family goals as well as individual goals. We use our vision boards as the "No Excuse Zone."

I remember for my best friend's Jill's thirtieth birthday, she wanted to travel to Paris. I told her, let's do it. Prior to the trip, my daughter Jasmine, who was very young at the time, was watching me pack and said, "Mommy, I want to go with you." I told her she couldn't go with me this time, but I promised her when she turned sixteen that I would take her. At that moment, she left the room and added it to her goal poster. Anytime we were out shopping, she would ask me to buy her pictures of Paris. When Jasmine turned sixteen, and since I am woman of my word, any guesses where we went? Yes, Paris! The smile on Jasmine's face is one that I will never forget. Even prior to the trip, when applying for her passport, she had this twinkle in her eye as if to say, I love my life. Always write the vision and make it plain. That's what the Bible instructs us to do.

At age thirteen, Jasmine had a monumental opportunity to travel to California for her first modeling gig. Were we nervous for her to travel alone? Of course, but my husband and I knew this was an important opportunity. While we both had scheduling conflicts, we knew she was in good hands with close friends. For me, it was reminiscent of when I was thirteen and traveled alone without my parents for the first time. That was when I gained my love for travel and I suspect it was the same for Jasmine. My mother traveled; she encouraged me to travel and see the world, and now I'm doing the same with my children.

Of course, Jasmine's trip influenced my younger children as well. My youngest daughter, Jade wants to go to Mexico. My son Jevon wants to travel to Dubai! Jasmine wants to travel to Australia. Can you say wow? My kids are big thinkers and dreamers. While most kids want tangible items, my kids value travel and all the rich experiences it provides. My husband and I think it's important to show them how to set goals. A life without goals is an empty existence.

My Mary Kay business has taught me the importance of making vision boards. In my Mary Kay business, I developed a passion to win by setting goals. My children have seen me set goals and achieve them. They have also seen me set goals and not reach them. Interestingly enough, they have never judged me if I missed the goal, but they would tell me, "Mom, it's okay. Remember you taught us the goal never changes just the timing of the goal. See, the goal always remains the same, so set another date, Mom!" This makes me feel wonderful as a parent when they encourage me. In my house, we are "team no excuses."

Encourage Yourself

In my home, we are constantly encouraging each other. I write positive quotes on my children's bathroom mirrors. Sometimes, I make them write out positive affirmations to say daily. I explain to them that you will have people who don't believe in you or your dreams and I encourage them to block out the negative voices and to record their own voice saying positive things, and play it at bedtime or before big events. In the age of modern technology, we have no excuse not to use technology in a good way.

#Tishtalk

What's your affirmation? Where's your positivity? Do you have a vision board? Craft one right now. Make sure you have a good time while doing it. When you're done, write out your affirmation. Don't worry, you'll edit it over time. When you use a positive affirmation, one that reflects gratitude and establishes a goal you wish to meet, you are clearly showing your faith to the universe on what you expect to happen. Go for it. Do it right now … or should I say, write now? As you meet the goal, find something else, and write a new one. Your affirmations can be altered daily … even hourly … if it helps you reach your goals.

_____
_____
_____
_____
_____
_____
_____
_____
_____
_____
_____
_____
_____
_____
_____
_____
_____
_____
_____
_____
_____
_____
_____
_____
_____
_____

#Tishtalk

What's on your vision board? What's your timeline to reach your goals?

_____

_____

_____

_____

_____

_____

_____

_____

_____

_____

_____

_____

_____

_____

_____

_____

_____

_____

_____

_____

_____

_____

_____

_____

_____

_____

_____

_____

8

THE "WALK-IN" CLOSET

As you know by now, I am a fashionista. I love all things fashion. As a child, I always gave advice to my peers, parents, and friends. I guess you could say I was grown before I was grown. I was never a buttinsky, but I would enjoy helping people anyway that I could. I think this is why my Mary Kay business is a perfect fit for me. It has allowed me to help women all over the world reach their goals. Let me tell you, lipstick on a woman means more than just colored lips. It can give her confidence and the courage to walk into a room full of dragons and slay them all! It can even put a special smile on her husband's face as she enters the room.

Speaking of rooms and special smiles, what's your favorite room in your house? Family room? Kitchen? Bedroom? As a mother of seven children ranging from young adulthood to tween years and a loving wife to a successful business owner, some people would assume that my favorite room would be the kitchen or bedroom. Wrong. My absolute favorite room in my house is my bedroom walk-in closet. One of my requirements for our new home was a huge walk-in closet. Of course, you would expect a fashionista like me to need a walk-in closet, but I need it for something else too. Clothes and shoes are not the only thing I like to mix and match while in the closet. Yes, I like "it" in the closet. You know "it". The same kind of "it" Stella found in Jamaica when she met

45

Winston, and he turned out to be that special chocolate that was good for her lips, hips, and thighs.

It's every woman's fantasy to have a huge walk-in closet. Many people would love a big walk-in closet. The walk-in closet signifies you have made it, or you've arrived. You have room for all your amazing clothes, shoes, and storage for other personal items. Honey, you can go in there and do your makeup if you have a vanity chair and mirror set sitting there. You can play, pray, and meditate too. Have you seen the movie *War Room*? Well, you can even have a prayer room, all in your walk-in.

Whatever you need to do, it starts with that walk- in closet. At least in my mind it does. Yes, you normally have to have your clothes in the closet, but did you know you can spice up your love life by being creative? For example, you can have dinner in your walk-in closet. Simply, throw down a blanket and have a picnic basket ready, then after eating, you can move to the bedroom. Or maybe not. Your choice. You can stay and play a little game of strip poker without the poker. The goal is to be liberated and think outside the box. In the age of quarantine, anything goes.

After a long day of work, I love to change the script by helping my husband slip into something more comfortable. He has to go in the closet anyways. Why not meet him in there and help him unwind from a long day of decisions, customers and demands. In the walk-in, I am not his wife but his lover who makes sure all his needs are met. I call it giving him "treatment" and the "treatment" is just what the doctor ordered. Sometimes, I am the choreographer. Directing his moves to mine. Slow and steady. Hot and heavy. Guiding him to his grand finale. Sometimes, he is the chef. Making his requests known. Depends on the mood. Sunny side up or over easy. Never the same dish twice.

As active parents and business owners still very much in love, we make time for each other. The key to staying in love is to never stop dating each other. My husband and I enjoy our date nights. It feels good to spend quality time with my best friend. We spend time alone holding hands, gazing into each other's eyes, and touching. Lots of touching. We also use that time to talk about us—our hopes and dreams for our family. If you want your relationship to work, you have to work for it.

Now some of you may be scowling right this moment. But Tish ... what if I don't have a husband? What if I only have a boyfriend ... or ... even no one? What then? Was I supposed to just skip this chapter?

Of course not. It doesn't matter if you don't have a second person in your life. There's you. Work on the relationship that you have with yourself. Have that dinner in the closet with you? How often have you done something wild and crazy and loving and supportive for yourself? I have a friend who always says never say something to yourself you wouldn't say to your best friend. I say, always treat yourself like you are your best friend.

Maybe you don't have a significant other, but do you have a child? Or a best friend? A parent? Someone with whom you share every aspect of your inner self? Someone you rely on, and who relies on you too? Then work on that relationship just as hard as if it were a marriage. No one should sit at the table of life by themselves. No one should choose to be on their own. Embrace the people who are in your life and build stronger bonds with them. You're never going to regret the love you give. It's the best investment you can make for your journey. You'll always get back tenfold of what you put out into the universe. I promise.

#Tishtalk

Who is your person? What can you do for them? I don't care if it's a husband ... child ... parent ... friend ... or yourself. Write that person's name on this page. Record who it is. Decide how you can form a better bond with that person. How can you build on what you have with them? You can soar so much higher when you have a foundation of standing on someone else's sturdy shoulders. Do it and do it today.

_____

_____

_____

_____

_____

_____

_____

_____

_____

_____

_____

_____

_____

_____

_____

_____

_____

_____

_____

_____

_____

_____

_____

9

BE A BUSINESSWOMAN AND NOT A BUSY WOMAN

GROWING UP, I loved going to church. Of course, we went to church on Sundays, but any other time I could go, I went. I loved all the special services–revivals, church anniversaries, Men's Day, Women's Day. I loved church. My mom never had to beg me to go. I would wake up willingly on Sunday mornings.

I am sure this is where I gained my passion for ministry and community events. I watched my mom and my Aunt Mae work in the church tirelessly. They did it all with a smile and were so gleeful. I can still hear them saying, "Serve the Lord with gladness." Did I mention the amazing Sunday dinners? Both my mom and Aunt Mae could throw down in the kitchen. Every Sunday we would go over to Aunt Mae's house to eat dinner, and she always cooked more than enough for the whole neighborhood.

Aunt Mae is truly our "Big Momma." She's considered the matriarch who keeps the family, on my Mom's side, together. She's like my mom's second mother but really her real mom, because she took her in and raised my mother. We all love and respect my Aunt Mae. This woman has never missed a birthday and she gives out gifts (expensive gifts to all of her children, grandchildren, great-grands and even now there are great-great-grands). She taught me how to just sit and spend time with Jesus. When I need to get away and just to get back to my roots, I will go over my Aunt Mae's house and all is well, once we talk about the goodness of the Lord. We can talk about God, Morning, Noon and Night I love to sit with her to gain knowledge and wisdom.

It wasn't until I went to college that I met another woman who would change and define my life in the way that my mom and Aunt Mae had. Mrs. Ann Shears was and still is my *shero*. This dynamic woman took me under her wing and taught me the foundation of business.

I met her as a young, single, and free college student at North Carolina Agricultural and Technical State University or more commonly and affectionately known as NC A&T. The school spirit at A&T is unprecedented. Yes, I'm biased but so is anyone who has ever experienced Aggie Pride. The annual homecoming is literally known as the GHOE, Greatest Homecoming On Earth. To all of my friends who attended other Universities, just don't argue with me, it is the *truth*. Now moving on ...NCA&TSU helped me grow me up in such a productive way.

I was there on a scholarship, and Mrs. Shears was my accounting instructor. It was a challenging class and I needed some extra help, and Mrs. Shears being one of the dedicated accounting instructors on campus, started tutoring me outside of class. I would go to her house and she would say I'm going to teach you about how to manage all this money you are making on campus without bankrupting your business. God has a sense of humor because again he placed an awesome professional businesswoman in my path to teach me about Money Management and how to become more business savvy. I like to say Mrs. Shears was really responsible for Jevon and I being married. I would confide in her even after I graduated and moved back to Charlotte. The day I moved back, I had a Mary Kay event in Charlotte. The day I met Jevon, I was stopping to get food for myself and Mrs. Shears. Most people don't know this, but she and Mr. Arlie Shears told me that if that man wanted my hand in marriage, he needed to prove it. They told me that I was not moving in with him until he did so. Shortly after that, Jevon proposed. We literally met and got engaged within six months and then we got married and didn't even tell anyone except our moms. I guess you can say that because of Mary Kay and Mrs. Shears and I both being hungry, I met and married my Prince Charming. Ladies, a lot more than makeup can come out of a starter Kit. I got a husband!

Mrs. Shears was also a successful Mary Kay Sales Director. I joined the business and literally sat at her feet learning about the business of makeup and business in general. I'm forever grateful to Mrs. Shears for introducing me to the Mary Kay business and "The Million Dollars Girlfriend's Club". This is a group of powerful and successful Mary Kay women who have earned at least $1Million in the business. This is when I met my shero, Dr. Gloria Mayfield Banks. She is the #1 Elite Executive National Sales Director for Mary Kay. Not only is she an internationally renowned motivational speaker, success strategist, and sales trainer; her alma mater, Harvard University teaches a case study regarding her sales success in Mary Kay. Dr. Banks' accolades are long and impressive, and she is passionate about coaching and training. Her energy is infectious. She taught me business skills, such as emotional management, money management, how to always to dress for success, (just like my dad would tell me) how important it is to have positive affirmations, and the importance of goal posters. As my National Sales Director, I am still learning from her today.

While in college, Mary Kay was a legitimate way for me to earn income and kept me from hustling the wrong kind of product. I grew up on the hard-knock west-side of Charlotte, North Carolina. Although sheltered, I was exposed to drugs and crime. As a child, I witnessed a murder. I saw a man pick up an axe and chop his former friend's head off. To survive, I quickly developed a tough outer shell.

I guess you could say that I was always a hustler. When I was a child, I sold my Halloween candy to my peers. I setup lemonade stands and yard sales. I loved having money, and I didn't mind working to get it. When I was 14, I was the neighborhood "kitchen hair stylist." You name the style and I could do it—finger waves, buns, and ponytails. I've always had a flair for the dramatic and passion for fashion.

Just like I was a natural seller, I've always been a leader. I was the captain of my basketball team in Junior High and High School. I ran track, played softball, and football, until my father made me quit football. He felt the game of football was much too rough for a girl, even though he was the one who taught me the game. I miss watching and talking sports with him. Studies have shown that there is a direct correlation between leadership and sports.

Mrs. Shears took all of my raw material and molded it into a workable product. From her, I learned how to mingle and network with business moguls. She taught me the art and necessity of team building. In Mary Kay, there is a saying, "Fake it until you make it." This means look, talk, and walk like a million bucks, until you get there.

I went from being an impressionable and inexperienced girl into a mature, charismatic businesswoman who would not take "no" for an answer. It wasn't just about selling lipsticks, eye shadows and foundation. It was learning how to sell anything. Mrs. Shears taught me the foundation of business. She taught me how to focus and have a clear vision for my business. So many women are busy with trying to create the illusion of a successful business that they forget to learn true business principles. Mrs. Shears taught me about sales, leadership and how to achieve a balanced life that works for me. My love for her is endless.

It is important to have mentorship in business. The first step to finding a good mentor is coming to terms with the fact that you can benefit from having one. Going it alone is admirable, but foolish. Someone, somewhere, has already been through the challenges you are facing. No matter how brilliant or business savvy you think you are, every business owner needs at least one good mentor.

Three Steps to Finding a Great Mentor

What makes a great mentor?

A great mentor will challenge you. They ask questions to guide you in the right direction. This person will not do the work for you, but acts as an advisor, as you do it on your own. After all, it is your company and not theirs. Don't be afraid to look for mentorship in non-conventional ways. Ask your colleagues and executive-team members for their point of view. In other words, embrace the learning opportunities all around you.

Find a good fit.

Does your mentor fit the business? Look for mentors you respect, and that have some insight into your type of business. If you don't know them personally, do your research. Find out if a meeting over coffee is better, or a simple phone conversation. In short, show them that you respect them enough to learn about them. Remember to respect their time; you need them, not the other way around.

Build a meaningful relationship.

A good relationship takes time to build. Just like any relationship, it takes time to learn about each other and to develop trust. One way to do this is to check in regularly by email. Mentors want to see your progress and know their input has been valuable. Keep the relationship going by asking at least one new question. Again, respect their time by keeping your in-person meetings brief. Be grateful and appreciative of them; they are giving you one of the most valuable things we all have, time. Don't ever waste it or make them feel like they are throwing away their wisdom on you.

Now that you have a business mentor, the next step is to get organized. There are plenty of ways to get organized. Remember some things work for some people and not for others. Organization will help you go from busy woman to businesswoman.

- **Use a Calendar**

It doesn't matter if it is digital or traditional, a calendar will help you stay organized. Businesswomen have a lot to juggle and maintain. You can use the app on your phone or the traditional planner, or even a hybrid method. When on the go, add appointments and reminders into your phone and once you are back in your office, write them into your planner. This helps you see the day, week, or month ahead.

- **Organize your notes**

When I am at a conference or seminar, I take notes. I try to keep them in a notebook or journal. I've noticed that there are others taking notes in electronic devices. Don't get me wrong, I do that too, but the key here is where you store the notes once the event is over. A good idea is to transfer the notes to Evernote, OneNote or google docs. You will probably have to find different methods until you find what works.

- **Business Finances**

Business finances can be complicated. There can be a right and wrong way to set them up. The right way allows you to automate almost everything. Any other method of compiling your finances that involves too much manual entry is wrong. The goal is to free up time and become efficient.

My husband and my mentors taught me to have separate business accounts because you don't want to mix the money for your personal accounts with your business accounts. This could bankrupt your business.

You'll need software. QuickBooks is great software and it's intuitive. At any rate, the software should have certain key features:

- Ability to link your business card and business accounts to your bookkeeping software. As long as your purchases are on your credit card or the debit card linked to your business checking, it will show up in your software.

- Ability to categorize purchases on an ongoing basis. Setup rules for what's what, and that's pretty much it. Periodically, you may need to run through it and ensure everything's categorized correctly.
- Make sure your software keeps track of how much you'll owe in estimated quarterly or yearly tax. You can have problems with the IRS if you don't pay your quarterly or yearly taxes.

Lastly, it's important to note that you don't have to be superwoman. If you need to hire someone to cook, clean or help organize, do it! A smart businesswoman knows that having a housekeeper or someone to come in and clean a few days, will free her up to work her business in order to be successful.

- **Business Sales**

People use the word hustler and back in the day "Hustler" had a negative connotation associated with it. Today if you're a hustler you are not looked down upon. It's smart to have a side gig, or another stream of income. It's really about having multiple streams of income. I love teaching women and men how to become multi-income makers. It's not about how much money you make, as much as it is about how much you keep of what you make... my children have worked for me and my husband's businesses for years and we pay them a salary. That's how you keep income and shelter it.

Below are some tips for selling:

- Sell yourself before you can sell anything else. The technique to selling yourself is to do it without sounding like you're doing it. Everything you do to sell yourself has to focus on what your customers need, want and value. Even when you're selling yourself, you're not doing that to make yourself look better; you're doing it so they understand what they get out of the relationship. They have to believe in you, before they believe in the product.

- Selling is about supply and demand. The terms supply and demand refer to the behavior of people as they interact with one another in markets. A market is a group of buyers and sellers of a particular good or service. The buyers as a group, determine the demand for the product, and the sellers as a group, determine the supply of the product.

- Let the customer know you appreciate their business. How people feel about you and their willingness to do business with you are closely related. In the eyes of your customers, it's all about them. If they feel valuable to you, and are treated with care and attention, they are more likely to become loyal. Always remember to thank the customer by using these tips:

- Greet your client by name.

- Express your gratitude and clearly state why you're sending the email or making the phone call.

- Include details about why you enjoyed your experience with this customer (be specific and personalize it as much as possible)

- Repeat your thanks.

- Close with a sign-off and sign your name.

- Anyone can be taught to sell. It is a skill you can learn. Yes, some people do have a more natural penchant for sales, but most of the really good ones are learners. Don't sell yourself short. You're capable of learning everything you need to know to be a massive success – and quickly.

Mary Kay has afforded me a comfortable lifestyle. With Mary Kay, I sell quality products, meet amazing people from all over the world, and drive free cars. I have learned from the best how to sell, but most of all, I've learned there is unlimited potential in sales. It has changed my life.

#Tishtalk

Why work for someone else making six dollars an hour, when you could be making $600 an hour in the field of skin care? Mary Kay is a network marketing company with wholesale volume over US $3 billion. The company has been in business since 1963. Consultants all over the world enjoy the benefits of selling Mary Kay.

Tishtalk

How do you stay organized? What software do you use to take notes or organize your finances?

_____

_____

_____

_____

_____

_____

_____

_____

_____

_____

_____

_____

_____

_____

_____

_____

_____

_____

_____

_____

_____

_____

_____

_____

_____

_____

_____

START TRIPPING

ALMOST TWENTY YEARS AGO, my husband promised me that he would take me on vacation at least every three months. While some of those vacations have been stay-cations or quick getaways, he's kept his promise. We both love to travel and finding new adventures has kept our marriage exciting and romantic. We work hard, but we play even harder. We've traveled to numerous countries and cities, I've lost count, but I hold all the memories very dear to my heart.

Travel exposes me to other cultures and exquisite foods. I love to try new foods. I'll try anything at least once. The reason that I have a passion for people is I encounter interesting people in the interesting places – and we talk.

I've had my passport for over twenty years. My passport is filled with stamps, and my goal is to expose my children to traveling as well. We started taking them with us on trips when they were very young. In most cases, they request trips as birthday presents instead of the normal-type presents. We're happy to oblige because this exposes them to other cultures and ways of life, and gives them understanding. It teaches them about diversity – something I feel everyone can learn to their benefit.

When I was a college student, I had a chance to go study abroad as an exchange student. I lived in San Jose, Costa Rica. I lived with a Costa Rican family and it was one of the best experiences of my life. The unofficial slogan of Costa Rica is Pura Vida meaning "pure life." The culture is very laid back and the natural surroundings are breathtaking. It's one of the most beautiful countries in Central America. There are towering volcanoes, liberal rainforests, exotic marine life, and cascading waterfalls. I vowed I would come back.

My return to Costa Rica was extra special because I traveled with my daughter Jasmine. She was in college, and it was her birthday trip. It became an all-girls trip that included one of my dearest friends and her teenage daughter. No stone was left unturned. We swam, biked, shopped and horse backed. We dined in all the best restaurants, enjoyed the spas, and meditated near the water. We got it in! The best part for me was seeing the smile on Jasmine's face.

When Jazz turned sweet 16, we took a trip to Paris. She was so excited. In fact, we both were. I was excited to show her a good time. We definitely left our mark in Paris. Jazz's next voyage? She wants to go to Australia when she graduates college and becomes Dr. Jazz. Of course, her younger siblings have already put in their graduation trip orders too! In fact, Jevon Junior has requested to go to Dubai. He graduates October 2021. Prayerfully, we'll oblige.

As I mentioned before, most of this book was written while traveling the world. I love what traveling does for my mind. There is nothing more inspiring than writing near a waterfall or ocean side.

· · ·

In this life, I've had many ups and downs. I've had to start over more times than I can count. In all honesty, looking back I wouldn't change a thing. In fact, I'm grateful that some things didn't work out the way I once wanted. With each bounce back, I have learned that trouble doesn't always last, but tough people do. Every time I thought I took a loss, God blessed me with something better. If I was booked for an event and it was canceled, God would bless me with another trip or business venture, all expenses paid.

The Top 5 reasons why you should travel:

1. To get out of your comfort zone

Whenever you feel like you are not growing or you're in a rut, take a trip. We learn the most when we are in uncomfortable, unfamiliar positions. Being in a new place with new surroundings, forces you to connect with people despite differences. You become a smarter, more competent individual.

2.You will develop cultural awareness

When you visit a country or region, you learn first-hand about the culture. As a businesswoman, I pay close attention to the culture around me. I focus on what matters to the natives and what doesn't. For example, in Costa Rica, the term "manana" is used frequently. The literal translation is "tomorrow", but in most cases, this could mean in a few days. It's a very laid back culture, and you have to learn to adjust.

3. Traveling increases confidence

As you conquer the obstacles of learning to ask for directions in a foreign language while in a foreign country, you are building confidence. Actually, you increase confidence traveling the United States. I have learned so much traveling this wonderful country. I have navigated the subways in the Northeast, the trains in the New England states, and the spider maze interstates on the west coast. And most importantly, there is no such thing as sweet tea north of Virginia.

4. Become immersed in a second or third language

Here in the United States, we don't necessarily need to learn another language. One could successfully argue that we're quickly becoming a country in need of learning other languages. Those in Europe have quite an advantage because they are adjacent to countries that speak different languages. Living abroad is one of the best ways to learn a new language. You are forced to practice the language daily.

5. Valuable opportunity to network

I have worked and studied abroad and made some valuable networking opportunities. Making friends abroad can prove to be worthwhile. I have so many wonderful friends spread across the world; I'm never in lack when I need an escort or host. Traveling has definitely increased my customer base. When my friends ask me to come visit them, I always ask them to have a girlfriends' night, so that I can bring some Mary Kay products. It turns into a skin care party, and my trip has just become tax deductible. Can you say write off? I did say that I was an entrepreneur and businesswoman, right?

No amount of business travel will ever outweigh the benefits of family vacations. Family travel is a way to teach our kids about the world beyond Charlotte, NC. With a large family, travel can be pricey, so we plan our trips months and sometimes, at least a year ahead. Here are some tips to save money for a family vacation and how to get the whole family involved.

Track Your Spending to Find Ways to Save Money.

Write down all of your expenditures for a week or two and look for patterns. Do you always eat out on Thursdays because those are busy days? Next time make a double-batch meal another night, to save on takeout costs. Are you surprised by how much money you spend on bottled water? Buy a refillable water bottle instead.

Get the kids involved.

Have the kids help save. After all, when they are involved with saving for a vacation it gives them a sense of ownership. Short-term, it helps them understand how much things cost. Long-term? It gives them the financial skills to understand how to work toward a goal. Older kids can put away a set amount per week from jobs; mid-age-range kids can put coins in a jar with a picture of your vacation destination on it. Younger kids can make choices: This candy bar now or saving for a beach trip.

If they get paid an allowance, add an extra chore where the money goes straight to their vacation-spending fun money. Let them run a candy store or make bracelets to sell. The more the kids are a part of the process, the more it will feel like a team effort.

Tighten Up Your Grocery Budget.

Look at your grocery budget. While it may not be the "lowest hanging fruit" for everyone, most folks could knock $20 or so off their grocery shopping trips. There are several ways to cut your grocery budget.

- **Meal planning.** Having a weekly or monthly meal plan will help you to overlap ingredients and cut down on food waste.
- **Low-cost meals.** Examining the cost per meal can help you to slim up your grocery store spending. Lower cost meals that include pasta or rice with less protein can free up extra money to go to vacation savings. Suddenly, that $10 pack of chicken is making 4 meals instead of 2.
- **Go generic.** Taste test some store brands vs. name brands and see if there are lower cost options you can work into your pantry. If

your children are the way my kids are, they probably won't go for this option. My children really don't like leftovers, but they eat them. No wasting in the Mciver Household.

- **Buy in bulk.** Single use items like school snacks for kids, cost more when packaged individually. Purchase reusable pouches and use them for applesauce and yogurts in lunches.
- **Make your own.** You would be surprised at how easy it is to make some basics like bread and yogurt. For us, the cost savings on these two items we burn through was mind boggling. I can make bread for 53 cents a loaf and yogurt at less than $2 for 5 quarts.

Don't Buy. Borrow or trade instead.

Get in the habit of borrowing items and using local resources instead of buying things. Instead of buying books for your kids, go to the library. Set a budget for how many books you'll purchase. Local libraries often offer discounted passes to local museums as well.

Cut the Gym Membership.

Did you know 6% of Americans spend money on a gym membership that they don't use? If you aren't hitting the gym, look into cancelling. It can be tricky with some contracts specifying life conditions you have to meet to back out, but persistence is key here. Keep asking and soon you'll be free of that monthly payment. Still need to work out? Look at cheaper options: online classes, or find an accountability buddy to take walks with and help. This was huge for my family especially in the middle of a pandemic; we started walking and exercising in our neighborhood and bonding as well, it has become more family time with a twist of competition. Friendly of course.

There are many more ways to save money for a family vacation. I've included just a few. I'm sure you and your family can come up with some new ways to save money to take that desired family vacation.

#Tishtalk

Where do you want to go the most? What languages do you want to learn? Write down at least five cities you dream of seeing. Write down at least one language you want to learn. Create your vision board and fill it with photographs of places in that city you wish to visit and place your photo with it. You'll get there if you see it. You'll love it, I promise.

_____

_____

_____

_____

_____

_____

_____

_____

_____

_____

_____

_____

_____

_____

_____

_____

_____

_____

_____

_____

_____

_____

_____

_____

_____

_____

_____

_____

_____

_____

One of the main reasons that I love to travel is to expose my mind and expand my views on life. I love experiencing other cultures. We must become expansive in our thinking if we want to experience new things, without being judgmental. Traveling enables you to meet new people and have new experiences. I've traveled extensively, and I wanted to share a little about a few of my favorite places. Here are my top 20 destinations:

#1 Greece was my favorite excursion mainly because the shopping was phenomenal. I recommend that everyone go to the see the Mediterranean Sea at least once. This was a trip I took with my girlfriends. The flight was long, but it was worth every mile. We visited the ancient ruins and because I studied Greek mythology, I've always admired the Greek God Zeus and the Goddess Athena.

#1 The Bahamas is tied with Greece because was also my #1 favorite place because of the wonderful memories that I hold near and dear to my heart. I have been 3 times. It's where my husband and I went on our honeymoon. No one knew but our Moms that we actually got married and flew to the Bahamas as "Mr. and Mrs. Mciver"!! We came back and didn't tell anyone for a year. For our actual first anniversary, we planned a huge wedding on the same exact wedding day we got married the first time. The Bahamas was the first place that I had traveled to, out of the country and required my passport. I love to get passport stamps.

We have taken the entire family on a cruise to the Bahamas and the kids had such a phenomenal time running around on the cruise ship and eating any and everything good time, and food that they wanted to eat. We love cruising because the food is plentiful.

The Third time we went to the Bahamas was an all-expenses paid by Mary Kay Company as a reward for accomplishing a major goal. The company flew us into Florida, and we got on a Royal Caribbean cruise ship. It was the most beautiful ship that we've ever been on. We didn't have to pay for anything. This was such a fantastic voyage with my Mary Kay Goalfriend sister Sales Directors and all of the husbands. We had a blast!

#2 Paris, France was absolutely amazing. They say it's for lovers, and it is very much so. It's rich with culture, and the food is amazing but most importantly the SHOPPING is on another level. I have traveled here twice and whether you go with your family or by yourself I would definitely recommend visiting. The first trip, I accompanied a friend. The day before I left for Paris, my daughter Jasmine said "Mom, I want to go with you." I told her that when she turned 16, I would take her to Paris. Wouldn't you know that for all those years she held on to that promise? When it was time for her to turn 16, I thought she was getting excited about her sweet sixteen milestone that allowed her to apply for her driver's license. No, she was excited to go to Europe. I was able to take her along with my girlfriend and her daughter. We toured museums, saw the Mona Lisa and the Lourve' and so much more. We ate dinner at the world-renowned Eiffel Tower, the Louvre and we visited Notre-Dame.

#3 Costa Rica - I had a chance to travel to Costa Rica twice. The first time, I studied abroad as a college student in San Jose. It is one of the most beautiful places in the world. I attended the Universidad Interamericana and I stayed with a Costa Rican family. As a student, I enjoyed the excursions, going to visit the tropical rain forest, botanical gardens, volcanoes, and bathing in the hot springs. I know that I keep saying this, but this is one of the most beautiful places that I have ever traveled to and the people are so friendly. The culture is rich, and the people are beautiful. I do speak a little Spanish, so I was ok. The second time I went, was when I took my daughter, Jazz, for a graduation trip. She wanted to go, and we had an eventful time. I totally love Latin America. What you need to know about Latin America is they have just two seasons, a rainy season and dry season.

#4 Hawaii – Wow, what can I say this trip? This island was hot, beautiful, and when you go to a luau everyone is your cousin. The colors are bright bold, and so radiant from the flowers, to the hot lava, to the tropical birds and fish. The energy of the people is laid back, surfing is amazing, and so is golf. Play a round of golf, visit the Honolulu Zoo, Hike Diamond Mountain. My husband and I did it all.

#5 Virgin Islands – You must go to feel the warmth of the water. The fish literally swim up to you and eat from your hands, and the water is crystal clear. The food and culture are amazing. You have to go during carnival. This is my family's and my vacation spot. We spent an entire week in St. Thomas then rode the ferry over to St. John for a day. This was one of the most memorable family vacations.

#6 Dominican Republic -- The people are beautiful, and the food is great. There's lots of shopping and beautiful paintings. The water was so clear, and all of the beaches were so beautiful.

#7 San Diego, California - We've traveled to California twice and both times it was to attend the Mary Kay Leadership Conference. The Company shut down the entire Universal Studios just so we (The Sales Force) could experience so much fun for free.

#8 Disney World - Orlando, Florida - We took the entire family to Magic Kingdom and Animal Kingdom. We had fun with the family -- riding rides, laughing, and taking pictures with Mickey and Minnie Mouse.

#9 Dallas, Texas - I love Dallas because it is where the Mary Kay Headquarters is located, and I have literally traveled there every year since I joined Mary Kay as a broke college student. When they say everything is BIG in Texas, it really is. The food is great, and the socialization is fun. I go there every summer in July.

#10 Miami, Florida - Four words, Party, Party Party, Party! The music, the entertainment, the food, and the beaches are like no other.

#11 New York City, New York - We love New York City! We have visited the Big Apple more than once, and we call these trips "The Mcivers take Manhattan". One of the main reasons I love New York is because it's fast paced. One of the main things that we told the kids is make sure you stick together and keep walking down the street because you will get a better deal. We love sightseeing --the Statue of Liberty, Hudson River, and Toy's R' Us.

#12 Las Vegas, Nevada – Sin City! The saying what happens in Vegas stays in Vegas definitely applies here. I had a blast. Vegas has something for everyone. If you like to gamble, the casinos are plentiful, but there are lots of places to dance and enjoy music, too. There are buffets in almost every casino. The hotels are picturesque. Spend some time in Bellagio, Bali's, Caesars Palace, Mandalay Bay, The Venetian, Treasure Island, MGM Grand, Paris, and Aria Resort. Lastly, the shopping is world class. Be prepared to stay up all night. Vegas never sleeps.

#13- Atlanta, Georgia – This was my first road trip with my husband. Since it is a quick getaway, we try to take our children at least once a year. It usually takes less than four hours to reach the Peach state. Atlanta is the hotspot for music and shopping.

#14- Phoenix, Arizona - The desert is amazing, and golfing is relaxing. If you go in the summer, be prepared for the dry heat.

#15 West Palm Beach, Florida - We took a family trip to West Palm Beach, and it's known for its upscale boutiques and irresistible beaches. We had some amazing food, too.

#16 Baltimore, Maryland – Nothing beats the harbor. There is shopping, music and food.

#17 Washington, DC – The nation's capital is a busy and vibrant city filled with historic buildings and museums. There is a strong music and art vibe. From DC, you can easily hop the train to other parts of the east coast.

#18 Minneapolis, Minnesota While everyone knows that Minneapolis is frigid in the winter, a major attraction is ice fishing. Don't be afraid to try something new.

#19 Chicago, Illinois – The windy city, Chi-town, or The 312; Chicago is rich in culture. There are so many museums and attractions. I personally enjoyed the Taste of Chicago—showcasing the diversity of Chicago's dining scene.

#20 Jamaica - I will never ever forget the four times that I have traveled to Jamaica, especially the first time which entailed fighting a madman for my life. I have since gone back, three times in fact. I had to go back to get my power back that the devil tried to steal from me. I let it go and let God take control over my fears, and the Comeback Queen emerged, and I will keep coming back from any obstacles that come my way. I would also like mention that the people of Jamaica are great people, and the culture is rich, and the food is spicy.

Pictures Say A Thousand Words

Here are some of my favorite pictures so you can see my life up close and personal.

<   Memories   ⚙

Thank you Daddy for always being my first love...You have
always believed in me and instilled great values in me!
Happy Father's Day! My escort for Miss Vanstory Hall @ NC
A&T SU! As soon as you heard that I was crowned Queen
 of my Dorm you headed to Greensboro to escort me!

Gloria Mayfield Banks

Horseback riding and Dune Buggie racing in the Dominican Republic!!

Lakertisha Slade- Mciver
Jul 16, 2015 · 👥

#ThrowBack Thursday #Focused #Keeping My Eyes on the PRIZE! #God got this

👍 Like   💬 Comment   ↪ Share

You, Jemica Atkins and 14 others

Lakertisha Slade- Mciver
Throwback Thursday

 Lakertisha Slade- Mciver
May 28, 2015 ·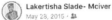

It was "All Good" just one month ago! Love chilling on ROOF
TOPS #MOUNTAINS views #Ocean Views #Greece #TBT
#Tanning #Mediterranean #Fun in the Sun on the island of
#Santorini #Vacation As often as you can
#Let'sGo...LIVING THE GOOD LIFE!

Final Assignment

We've talked about having a strong support base, driving out drama, creating good habits, and keeping your relationships spicy. We know that life can throw curve balls but it's up to you if you catch it, dodge or throw it back. It's up to you to plan your life. Write it down and execute!

ACKNOWLEDGMENTS

First and foremost, I want to give Thanks to God for giving me the strength, courage, wisdom and the wherewithal to actually write a book and finish this project in the middle of a pandemic. This book means so much to me; I'm a very passionate person and I want the words to JUMP UP off the pages and give you (the readers) LIFE. I want to thank my Family for always believing in me and allowing me to take time away from them to write and cultivate. Thank you for being a part of my creative design team and also the sacrifices that you've all made for me to finish this creative work. To Jevon - my Husband - you are the wind beneath my wings and to all of my children thanks for your words of affirmation and encouragement ~ you each represent a piece of my heart -we are a family – The Mighty Mciver and Always Mciver strong.

My sincere love and thanks to my mother, Mary Slade, and my beloved father, Herman "NIP" Slade, who always encouraged me to do my Best, Smile Big, Always, Always, Always, (He would give me my three "Always" every time). "Dress for Success" and when you walk in the room "Suck all of the air out of the room Tish"!! Well I am still doing just that, Dad. My father was my very best friend and he is still here in spirit and his energy lives on through his grandchildren. He loved his Grands!!

Oh, my Goodness, he would be very proud to know that I am an author now.

I want to thank my entire Mary Kay Team and my amazing unit "The Mciver Motivated Millionaires Unit" and the Magic Area Director's and Consultants for always encouraging me to WIN. I want to thank all of my family and friends who have always supported my vision.

Thanks, and gratitude to my love ones and friends for your patience and encouragement while I was in the trenches working on this book. I got your phone calls and text messages, but I had to go in the lab with my pen and pad and finish this book and not come up for air until it was all done. I pray that it blesses you like it has blessed me.

Thanks to my godmother Audrey, who helped raise me and my godsister, LaTonja. I appreciate the way you loved and cared for me from the time I was a small child, through growing up, college and even into adulthood, you've always treated me like I was your own child. I'm forever grateful. You taught me what it was to become a successful entrepreneur and because of your hard work and determination, that is where I get a lot of my grit, from just watching you build your real estate company and other businesses from the ground up. You helped me purchase my very first home and I will never forget our talks. I love you Momma, forever.

Special thanks to Harold Richardson, my godfather, who has always been there for me and my family since the very beginning. Thank you for encouraging me to be all that I can be, and your unwavering love and attention to my family! When I had no one to call, I knew that I could always call on you. I appreciate you more than you know.

Thanks to my very best friends in the whole wide world (5 Pack). Thank you Bestie, Marika McKie for helping me, (THE COMEBACK QUEEN), come back from Jamaica – I owe you everything. Thanks for being you- so driven, a passion for Fashion, and teaching me how to sew my first shirt in college -we really have been fashionistas way before then. Special thanks to My Best Girlfriends Jill, Letasha, Alesia, Tiffany, not just being my friends but my sisters. We have stood the test of time...from college 5 Pack to Motherhood, Marriages, and Making Money together. It's been over 25 years of solid sisterhood and I love and admire each one of you and your beautiful families. The joke was that I was going to have a beauty salon, because I loved fashion in college, and that I would be dressed up going across the yard to the Business Department for classes. Yep, I walked across campus in 3-inch heels and I wear them higher now, love my Stilettos! Y'all said that in college I would get married 1st and have the most kids and guess what ~ y'all we're correct because I love children. Jill, special thank you for being such a great friend to me and loving my entire family authentically and being Jasmine's godmother, we're Blessed to have you and Nia in our lives. Nia, thanks for always looking at me the way that you do, with such admiration. I love you, Niece. You will always be the 8th Mciver!

I want to acknowledge my niece who's also like a daughter to me-- Destiny you set the bar really high and thanks for inspiring your brothers and your cousin Jasmine and my other children. Because of you and your courage, academic achievements, intelligence and brilliance, you received a full ride to UNC Chapel Hill. The Family NOW understands what it means to strive for excellence because of you and your unwavering faith. Your mom asked me to help name you when you were born, and we knew then that you were destined for success ... thanks for being an excellent example and so super smart!

When you talk about a sister/ girlfriend that always looks out for you and always acknowledges her love and adoration, I could be speaking about the one and only, Lahari Jones. Our friendship over the last 20 years have meant so much to me and I appreciate you for calling me - to always check in and be present when my father passed away. It's like God allowed you to be my peace, and like a guardian angel, my protector during a very hard, awkward, and emotional time in my life. I will never forget you for helping me recover- you know the innermost secrets.

Thank you Regina Wims for being the biggest cheerleader for my family and a prayer warrior! You cover us all the time. Thanks for being my sister-in-Christ, and always sending packages for your nieces and nephew! We love You, Will, Chancellor and Josiah. God, thank you for allowing us to meet in Downtown Charlotte while she was on her cell phone.

Special thanks to my Selfish club sisters (who were all so Selfless). This was an organization that was started for women to celebrate one another, in a tight sisterhood, in a very sincere manner, with our accomplishments, and show self-love to each other - but most importantly, displaying self-love to oneself. Being selfish is not a bad thing, Lahari, Ebony, Reina, Alethia, Susan, Nichole, Schala, Clare, Altice, Cynthia, Iesha, and Traci

My childhood friends that grew up with me on West Blvd, I cherish every memory! From us walking up to Revolution Swimming pool, to the park across the street, to us riding our bikes through the path to go up to the grapevine store, or Mr. Rob's, to us playing in Sandhurst Apartments, or to walking to Barringer school to play a game Kick ball.

Thank you to my teachers in school that recognized that I was very different from the rest of the students – I've always had a free spirit.

I want to send a special thanks to Ebony Stubbs, who has always been the most genuine person that I know. Her smile resonates with everyone. She is a perfect example of professional, corporate Boss and Entrepreneur Boss babe. I listened when she needed a muse, and she allowed me to be her model in front of camera and I thank you for inviting me to a Mary Kay skincare pampering party in college. Thanks for introducing me to Shandi (Barksdale at the time) who is now married to the Honorable Pastor Adrian Starks - this is where I got my Mary Kay start and my Journey began. I am forever Grateful 🖤

Special thanks to my MARY KAY girlfriends, who understand me and help me believe that my confidence is off the charts. You'll pump me up, make me better, and feel more beautiful on the inside than outside. That's what makes me different, and makes me tick (I sell, teach and train women on Confidence.) The relationships that I have formed with you all are real and authentic ~it's with a great mix of the right ingredients such as love, support, adoration and encouragement that makes for great recipe of success! What are we cooking up today Ladies?

Thanks to my MK Best Friend Pink Cadillac Sr. Sales Director Liane Wall for your realness and your flair for the dramatics, like me! We are #TeamTOOMuch for a reason, and I appreciate my brother, Trevis Wall, and your children for adding to my life tremendously.

Thank you Lakeisha Chisolm for your Humbleness and Sassiness, (as well as your husband, Christopher and you beautiful children). Thanks Taunya Finley for always being willing to teach and train on the spot. Thanks to my Shine Bright like a Diamond girlfriend, CaRita Bailey, you know I love you.

A huge thank you to my Friend and sister Carolyn Muse - my prayer warrior girlfriend, and an amazing encourager. Thank you for all your words of positive affirmation that you continuously speak over me and my husband and my beautiful family. You remind us to #StayONTheHoneyMoon. Love you and Mr. Thomas Muse. You have been such a blessing since we met.

Thanks to Sales Director Mrs. Jacqueline Moore, who we all call "Momma Jackie" in the Pink Bubble of the Magic Area Family. You're truly special to so many – you're one of a kind! Your heart is so huge, and I love you for who you are. Thanks for your gentleness and warm smile, and at every Mary Kay event, I look for you.

To my California Sunshine, as I like to call her, Joy Tucker. I will never forget the day we first met, and we have been fast friends from that day forward. We were in the bathroom praying together at a Mary Kay event and now we talk, pray, train, encourage, educate and inspire our units together and we always exchange smiles, hugs and share laughs. We always have to see one another at our Mary Kay Conferences - at 1st God had it to be intentional for us to meet and now we make it our business to connect every year. I love you and your smile lights up the world. You have the sweetest voice and an even sweeter Sunny and Bright disposition.

Thanks to my true friend and sister, Mrs. Tabitha Albury, for being my 1st Offspring Sales Director. I appreciate your drive, your compassion, your love for teaching, your passion for people and we met because of Mary Kay - thanks to my brother Lenny and your children for being so remarkable!

Thanks to my Mary Kay Sales Director GoalFriends, that encourage me beyond makeup: Latricia Henry, Robyn Barnwell, Angela Tatum Morning, Lisa Charity. And for helping me break my own person belief barriers, thanks to Andre Charity, Michelle Calbert, Randell Calbert, Ebun Osaze and Mr. Asim Osaze - Watching you all transform the Mary Kay World has been Life Changing!!

Thanks to National Sales Director Sabrina Goodwin Monday, National Sales Director Emeritus Nora Shariff Borden, National Sales Director Natalie Jones, National Sales Director Crisette Ellis, National Sales Director Mia Mason, National Sales Director Candy D. Lewis for all of the LOC Training and just leading by example.

I can't mention Mary Kay without mentioning the energy in motion, Dr. Gloria Mayfield Banks. Thank you for always encouraging me to win and providing the foreword to this book. Your support means everything to me. Being one of your 1st Line Offsprings is monumental and I remember listening to tapes of you, and now I get to hear you up close and personal. My children grew up listening to you in my cars (back when we had cassette tapes) and then to the CDs, but now all we have to do is call you because your number is on speed dial and although you have shared the stage with Oprah Winfrey, John Maxwell and some of the greats, you will always be number one in my book. I love talking to you every week on our weekly conference calls. Thanks for being such an amazing mentor to me and so many others.

Thanks to Kings Park crew - you know who you are!

Most definitely Leslie Beatty, my girlfriend who could play football just as hard as me, back in the day and then turned into my college roommate. I remember our rap battles, and no one was fresher than us and I can still spit a hot 16 bars. I know you can too...Love you and my beautiful niece and nephew.

Thanks to my Favorite Principal and everyone else will agree with me, that Mr. Ken Wells was the most professional, coolest and laid-back educator, and THE BEST Principal ever. Thanks for believing in my vision, back in the day, when young BLACK girls were not supposed to have a vision or a voice - but you trusted your own judgment and allowed me to start an organization for our voices to be heard. You were open to a little black girl from West Blvd., who was trying to find herself, but just needed a platform to express my creativity. You never tried to put me in a box and so you listened to me that day, in your office, that we could find creative ways to express ourselves through dance and step team. Mr. Wells you created a safe place for us. That bond that we all formed back then with a lot of my friends from Carmel and South Meck High school; we're all still close, and for that I say thank you for believing in me and all of us.

Coach Troy Gaston – a special thank you for being an awesome mentor, coach and valuable friend to me and my entire family, you taught us things that I am still teaching my kids today.

Nefertari Benton, who inspired me to model at the young age of 13, and I appreciate momma Cynthia, who helped my love for traveling for allowing me to travel with y'all every year. Thank you.

Thanks to all of my childhood friends who attended Barringer Elementary - to Carmel Jr. Highschool (at the time) and then South Meck Highschool - the Track Team relay was explosive Jackie, Thelathia,

Tiffany, and Tish! I've always been a part of winning teams; our basketball squad was amazing and special. Thanks to Gail, Melissa, and Coach Troy Gaston.

Most of y'all don't know, but I get encouragement every day from Jevon Patterson! I really appreciate you, because you keep everyone on their toes, and you keep me LIFTED UP. You must always have a balcony person in your life and balcony people raise you up. Thank you always for singing my praises and acknowledging me for being a Fashionable Trendsetter and Fashionista. Thanks for your authenticity and your love ♥ and support of my family.

My NC A&T Queens: Lavondra, Leslie (my college roommate), Tomeka, Shanetta, Kyeshia, Tanya, Kenya, Brandy, Lashawn, Micky, Porsha, Tiffany, Karen, Donica, Felicia, Holly, Christy, Jocelyn, KD (Keisha), Ebony, L Evans Coley for keeping me covered in prayer. All of you will always have a special place in my Heart

Dr. Schenita Randolph, who has always been very inspiring, and such a phenomenal woman of God, and beautiful singer - Thanks for being who you are in my life. Thank you to your amazing husband, Dante and your beautiful children.

To my great friend, the Boss Chic herself, Ms. Ebony Moore. She was the loudest, most fabulous sister a girl could have, she was very charismatic and the life of every party and if there was a microphone anywhere, she was going to grab it and get the party lit. I miss you like crazy Girl and I remember no one could say my name like you-- L-A-K-E-R-T-I-S-H-A. You would pronounce every syllable, may you rest in Heaven.

Thanks to my Power Partner, Aderonke Dojio, who traveled from the United Kingdom to come visit with me and build our MARY KAY units, when she was pregnant with her son, Paul. Wow. I have so much respect for you and a great deal of love for you and your entire family – you're such a very powerful woman and such an amazing woman of God.

I want to thank my spiritual fathers, the late Dr. George Cook, and my Bishop, Dr. Walter C. Gwin, for nurturing my spiritual gifts and helping me identify my purpose in life, which is to encourage God's people and exhorting as well as empowering them to prosper.

Thank you Bishop Gwin For helping me get through one of the most difficult times in my life, when my father was ill and passed away. You were right there from the beginning to the end and I will never forget that. I appreciate you more than you know. Thanks for being my family.

Thanks to Elder Earlene Edwards -Beautiful Woman of God - for all of your prayers. Thank you for being a prayer warrior and a great counselor. I love you to life, Leo Twin.

My Glam Squad Iesha Gist, Tanica Gist, and Anaja Marie Barksdale (makeup artist and cousin), my wardrobe stylist and personal fashion designer - Tamara Shanell. Y'all keep me Flyyyy and my stylist, friend and family, Derikus Crawford and his crew – Sonya and Steven. I love y'all so much, thanks for helping me get ready for my Book Cover at the very last hour.

Thanks to Kevin Douglas for a great photo shoot. I appreciate your attention to detail.

Angela Davis, thank you our fireside chats, at all times during the day but especially in the mornings when we were both fresh from meditating.

Thanks, Tamara Shanell and Schala Harper, for all of our prolific conversations and helping understand that being different is ok and being esoteric is on another level.

To my book execution team - who helped me throughout this process. Your guidance and leadership made this very easy --- Jelani Hill, founder of BrandUScript (Publicist and Brand Manager) and you claim that I'm a Business Guru, and thanks to Lucinda Dunn-Page of Dunn Deal

Publishing, for staying up with me late nights and early mornings while consulting during the writing of this book.

Thanks Dr. Joy Alston and Minister Dana Williams, for always covering me and my family in prayer and helping me give birth to this book and coin the phrase "Not without my Lipstick!" and "Put some lipstick on and Go Run the World".

Shout out to All of My Family including Aunts, Uncles (John Slade and Lonnie Davis) cousins, Friends, and Framily- which are friends that became family. Thanks to Tiawana Brown for being so bold and beautiful. Thanks for standing up for justice; continue to allow God to use you and I love you so much - thanks for your encouragement and kind words always #T-NT coming soon - Keaton, Sharon Martin, Bj, Tyler, Kiki, Gaynelle, Tyrone, TEMNEBI, Dawn, Patricia Gaines, Derekia Slade, Shaye Moore and family, Lois Slade, Uncle John Slade, Aunt Jennie, Lois, San, Teresa, Lonnie, Jackie, NKenge Ayoka, my nephews DJ, Dillion, Ms. Pricilla Pots, and LaTara Beasly, Ms. McKie, Polly, My cousin Kimberly Ratchford, my favorite cousin who's also my daughter Jasmine's godmother.

Thank you to my church family for their prayers and support. The 1st church that I ever attended was Greater Mount Saini Baptist Church; this has been my family church for over 60 years. Dr. George Cook married Jevon and I. When we decided 10 years later, as our family grew, that we were looking to expand our Spiritual knowing, we then we went to visit our current church and I understand why I have been planted at Spirit of the Word Church International. I am there because God placed me there, to be on assignment and be a chosen vessel to help fulfill his mission for sharing the love of Jesus Christ. I will continue to let his light shine through me. Thanks for allowing me to grow and bloom where I'm planted.

Last, but never least, thanks to my NC A&T family. I am sending out a big #AGGIEPRIDE!

The One, the Only Lakertisha Slade Mciver

Lakertisha Slade Mciver was born and raised on the west side of Charlotte, North Carolina, her family and friends refer to her as Tisha, the "Diva". However, everyone that crosses her path will agree that she has the most genuine spirit. Ever since she was a young girl, she has always had a passion for modeling, the fashion industry, traveling around the world and her strongest passion was being a successful Entrepreneur.

She graduated from high school with honors and went on to North Carolina Agricultural and Technical State University, again with honors, and earned her Bachelor of Science Degree in Business Management. As a Senior in College, she obtained a chance to travel and study abroad as an exchange student in Central America. She attended Universidad Interamericana, in San Jose Costa Rica, where she studied Spanish, International Business Management and Marketing.

While in college she found excitement in pursuing her own business with Mary Kay Cosmetics. She was on the fast track and became a Mary

Kay Sales Director in record time, leading her personal team and Unit members to earning cars, becoming top sellers, and empowering lives for the better. Mary Kay has allowed her and her family to live a lavish lifestyle, which she continues to operate in the spirit of excellence while teaching her family the value of having faith and integrity. After graduating she worked as a banker, teacher, and her main focus has always been to continue to build strong connections and relationships through Mary Kay. She also helps her husband in their family business of successfully owning and operating Donna K's Southern Cooking, formerly known as Floyd's Soul Food Restaurant, of 25 years.

She enjoys ministry as well as volunteering in her community. She works red carpet events, models at fashion shows, and is also a phenomenal make-up artist for over 23 years.

People say that her life is like a juggling act, and she does an excellent job of balancing her career and her family of thirteen people, including maintaining her personal and social Life. She is married to the love of her life, Jevon Mciver, and they have seven beautiful children and six grandchildren, but she flinches at the word Grandma … she is called "GLAM-MA or Gi-Gi!" As the matriarch of the family, she is a devoted wife of twenty-three blessed years, loving mother, and caring friend.

Her principles that she lives by is putting GOD first, family second, and career third. She has received many accolades and awards in her Mary Kay career, such as number one salesperson for her unit that was ranked number eight in the nation out of fifteen thousand units.

Since she was a little girl she would confess that she was going to become a millionaire; due to her unwavering faith in God, her focus, and true dedication to her dreams, she is well on her way! Her enthusiasm is truly contagious, her ambition is real, and she has a natural ability to lead and motivate people. Tish loves all people and continues to live her life by the Golden Rule, which is "Do unto others as you will have them do unto you."

Her favorite quotes are: "Never let people put your 8x10 vision in a 5x7 frame." and, "When you know what you want and want it bad enough, you will find a way to get it … no excuses!" Her favorite Bible passage

(KJV) is Jeremiah 29:11: "For I know the plans that I have for you, declares the Lord, plans to prosper you and not to harm You, Plans to give you hope and a future."

Made in the USA
Columbia, SC
28 October 2024

44871744R10069